FREELANCE
YOUR
WAY
TO
FREEDOM

ALEXANDRA FASULO

FREELANCE YOUR WAY TO FREEDOM

HOW TO FREE YOURSELF FROM THE CORPORATE WORLD
AND BUILD THE LIFE OF YOUR DREAMS

WILEY

Published by John Wiley & Sons, Inc., Hoboken, New Jersey.
Published simultaneously in Canada.

For general information on our other products and services or for technical support, please contact our Customer Care Department within the United States at (800) 762-2974, outside the United States at (317) 572-3993 or fax (317) 572-4002.

Wiley publishes in a variety of print and electronic formats and by print-on-demand. Some material included with standard print versions of this book may not be included in e-books or in print-on-demand. If this book refers to media such as a CD or DVD that is not included in the version you purchased, you may download this material at http://booksupport.wiley.com. For more information about Wiley products, visit www.wiley.com.

Library of Congress Cataloging-in-Publication Data

Names: Fasulo, Alexandra, author.
Title: Freelance your way to freedom : how to make 7 figures online, free
   your mind, and work from anywhere in the world / Alexandra Fasulo.
Description: Hoboken, New Jersey : John Wiley & Sons, Inc., [2023] |
   Includes bibliographical references and index.
Identifiers: LCCN 2022029593 (print) | LCCN 2022029594 (ebook) | ISBN
   9781119893233 (hardback) | ISBN 9781119893257 (adobe pdf) | ISBN
   9781119893240 (epub)
Subjects: LCSH: New business enterprises. | Businesswomen. |
   Entrepreneurship. | Gig economy.
Classification: LCC HD62.5 .F368 2023 (print) | LCC HD62.5 (ebook) | DDC
   658.1/1—dc23/eng/20220801
LC record available at https://lccn.loc.gov/2022029593
LC ebook record available at https://lccn.loc.gov/2022029594

Cover Design: Paul McCarthy

SKY10036130_092222

*To my momager, who has played both mom and dad
to my sister and me—thanks for teaching me to rub some dirt on it,
get back up, and go out there and crush my dreams.*

CONTENTS

FOREWORD

I'm currently sitting at the highest café in the Chamonix ski resort, facing Mont Blanc, the second-tallest mountain in Europe, and drinking hot wine as I write this.

My workload these days is around five hours a week, totally remote.

My computer, camera, sometimes WiFi, and power are literally the only things I require for my work.

I'm 33, a multimillionaire, an entrepreneur running multiple businesses, and an investor in real estate (11 dwellings at present count), precious metals, crypto, fine art, businesses, and more. Technically, I could be completely retired as my passive income from just my properties is enough to cover all my expenses, which is 100 percent hands off. Retirement is not something I seek, however.

Obviously, this isn't a position that I landed into straight away. I had to start at the bottom of the entrepreneurial ladder.

And it started with a simple idea: I will learn to work remotely. There is no plan B.

I knew my life was going to be filled with endless adventures and travel, and I knew a job would get in the way of that. And I wasn't about to allow some silly need for a paycheck get in the way, just so that I could feed myself.

And I meant that. I wasn't going to have a plan B. That was never an option—no matter how long it took, no matter if I had to eat baked beans for years, no matter if I had to sleep on friends' couches without a place to call my own. All my energy was directed at this goal.

I started working in bars, juggling four waitress/bartender jobs at once while I was studying marketing (one of the most important skills that helped me get to where I am).

Bar jobs covered my living expenses while at the same time freeing up my brain space so I could return home after work and study the necessary skills I needed to make an online business work.

When I tell people that I worked 16-hour days in my twenties, people often laugh, don't believe it, or romanticize the idea that perhaps I was making little YouTube videos or reading up about how social media works.

Well, those were components of it, but so was cleaning up drunk people's vomit in the bar bathroom at midnight.

The entrepreneur's journey is never pretty. It certainly tests you and makes you truly realize that there is no job beneath you if it's helping you on the journey of becoming eventually free.

And yes, I understand that some will need to work three jobs just to support their household, as there is no spare time or money to try to focus on growing a side business for them.

That is a chapter in the life of that person, who isn't in the incredible position you are in right now, just *trying* to understand remote work by holding this book.

And that's why *we* need to pursue our dreams, for us and for them.

For the people who right now cannot make this lifestyle a dream of theirs, perhaps eventually your remote work will be so successful that you'll be able to give back and help to free others from the burden of just having to exist day to day, with no potential of future planning.

That's something I have the opportunity to do these days, thanks to my work that blossomed beyond my wildest dreams.

But then, there's also the crew that will shun any mention of the drastic personal responsibility like the responsibility this book will demand that you have in order to make the entrepreneurial lifestyle work for you, because it's an uncomfortable truth for many, in a far too comfortable world.

If I had a cent for every excuse or comment I read from people trying to explain why they couldn't make their dream come true, I would have been a multimillionaire at a much younger age. That shield keeps these people hidden from the demand to give it everything they've got in order to be great.

And so, don't be that person. Don't complain that you can't have your dream life if you truly realize that you're just lying to yourself. You're literally just hurting yourself by trying to protect your lies.

Okay, now back to the story of how I got here.

Following my vomit-cleaning, study-filled years, I ended up getting a job as a marketing coordinator, which progressed into a marketing manager position. This experience lasted two years, and it was one of the greatest jobs I could hold because it taught me even more about what I needed in order to make my own online business work.

My eyes were always on the prize.

My job taught me the value of direct response marketing and the value of selling online education, which is something that people always seek, something they always need, something that you get to price yourself without permission, and you have a global market to sell to, 24 hours a day.

It unlocked my eyes to creating a great product, building a community around that interest, and marketing it over and over, with the sales coming in hour after hour, day after day, including when you sleep.

So what is the core of my business now?

Exactly what I learned during my long, cold, gray office years, which is selling digital products.

Through what I learned during every single job I ever had, including the bar jobs, I have now created and mastered my go-to formula, launching very successfully five times now, selling upwards of $5 million in revenue, most of that being pure profit.

This has been repeated in a vast range of interest areas as well.

This all might sound very simple to you, or perhaps you're rolling your eyes thinking, "I'm sure it worked for you, but it won't work for me."

Sure, you can say that to yourself, and it will be true.

I instead chose to see other people living this type of life and seeing it as evidence that this world was meant for me, and that if other people could do it, so could I. All I needed to do now was to skill myself up within the necessary areas to get to my goal of working wherever in the world I wanted to.

I absorbed every drop of information around me to see if it was suitable for my online monetization journey, chose to be very selective with my time, and unfortunately made those sacrifices not to go out and party because there was nothing tastier than freedom, which was in the near(ish) distance.

Pair that with my unshakable confidence that I would succeed, with no backup plan.

And I got there.

This is why this book you're about to read is so significant.

While it took me from the age of 19 until 30 to figure out the formula, which is replicable within my field, category, and interest area and which more or less guarantees results, I know it probably didn't have to take this long.

I never had a manual. I never had a road map.

When I started my journey, the idea of working online and living wherever in the world I wanted to, for as long as I wanted, simply was not a real possibility. It was inconceivable.

In fact, people laughed at it and at anyone trying to pursue this world.

There were hardly any examples of people living this way because, indeed, the internet wasn't as saturated as it is today—a full, wonderful, endless library to help you grow, and accessible at your fingertips.

I used to have to fight with people, saying how outdated the 9-to-5 office work model was and that people need to work less and be able to work remotely in order to be happier and more productive.

And then the COVID pandemic hit, and it swiftly shifted most people's perceptions from thinking this world was impossible to realizing it was actually a much better way of working.

But then people were left with the question of how to live this new lifestyle forever, maybe even wanting to become their own boss.

And how to start this journey?

That's why I'm thrilled you're holding this significant book in your hands from a woman who accomplished great success for herself at such a young age, defying all the odds to come out on top—someone who is living a life that almost everyone dreams of.

I personally never thought to create a road map for people interested in escaping the 9-to-5 grind and transitioning into their next remote work chapter.

My path wasn't smooth, and I wouldn't know how to put it into a manual.

But Alexandra Fasulo figured out the essential components you need to make this journey so much easier for you.

You're in amazing hands. Take notes and follow her guidance carefully, knowing that sometimes copying a strategy is the perfect thing to do until you work out your own spice in the recipe.

But the most important advice I have and always tell people is to please take action.

You don't need to take giant leaps daily. Small daily action and energy focus will get you there, I promise you.

This world *is* for everyone, and it *is* possible for anyone.

It doesn't require anything special of anyone except the dedication to make this goal happen.

Because the beautiful thing about the internet is that there is a market out there for everyone to sell anything.

If you can think it up, you can find it and sell it on the internet, whether it's being your own boss or finding a forward-thinking company to work for that encourages remote working and that you believe in.

People before you, like Alex and me, have made this reality possible for themselves, and you're not different from us.

The fact that you're holding this book shows you want this for yourself.

So strap in, baby, because your life is about to change significantly, and you can thank yourself for being brave enough to believe you can.

Now go out there and do great work.

—Sorelle Amore
CEO of sorelleamore.com

PREFACE

The remote work economy is a diverse and ever-expanding place with abounding opportunity, money, and interpersonal freedom. It's a place where you can be your own boss, open as many streams of income as you desire, and do it all from anywhere in the world. No senior manager is watching, waiting to scold you for forgetting punctuation in an email with a client. It seems almost too good to be true; it's like a futuristic workplace utopia.

From my experience over the past decade immersing myself in online marketplaces after quitting my job with no plan or money saved, I have found that the world of remote work is indeed some kind of a utopia, where you can trade hard work and commitment for unlimited freedom. It's a place where working smarter, not harder, is praised; where technology, automation, and virtual assistants can remove the traditionally long working hours while you unplug for the afternoon on some remote digital nomad island in Southeast Asia.

But not even I could fathom that kind of utopia after years of college and two different office jobs that groomed employees for a life of servitude. I slid right into the belief that I had to suffer in the name of responsibility as an adult, as if suffering was a normal exchange everyone had to engage in if they wanted to own a house, a car, and pay off their debt.

Boy, was I wrong, and the remote work economy spared no time in showing me that these beliefs were rooted in an old-school approach to work that was born out of the Industrial Revolution. This new kind of online, interdependent economy only wants one thing from you: accountability. It wants you to show up, with a laptop and WiFi, as you open your accounts to check in on your teams, clients, and software that does your work in the background. If you can manage to do that—and only that—you're going to be in luck. Suffering is not part of this process, and it's certainly not expected of you if you want to be successful with a few side hustles you only put 30 minutes into managing each day.

This book is not about getting rich quick or hacking hidden systems. It's about laying the foundation in the remote work economy that will help you achieve financial independence in a fraction of the time your corporate employer promised.

We will first look at the remote work economy as a whole and how to navigate it as a beginner, followed by breaking down the ins and outs of freelancing and how to leverage your own agency, which you manage from anywhere in the world. We'll go over the different places you can freelance and how to set yourself apart from the competition.

Next, we'll explore the systems you need to put in place, the discipline and mindset development that's required to be successful, and secret side hustle hacks that can help you scale to six figures during your first year in business. Lastly, we'll talk about money momentum, using your success to build a personal brand that branches off into more revenue streams, and we'll go over a final checklist that will set you up to build your own seven-figure online empire.

The concepts in this book are not hard to understand—I promise. Although the idea of remote work and all the hundreds of side hustles available to you today can seem overwhelming, this book is intended to make simple the very basics of making money reliably through the remote work economy. I will detail every single decision I made to go from unemployed to sitting at the helm of a seven-figure freelance writing and social media personality business today, so that you can replicate my remote work blueprint.

Enjoy the adventure as we set out together to help you reclaim your personal freedom.

ACKNOWLEDGMENTS

This book and the inspiration for it would not have been possible without the "squad" of my mom, sister, stepdad, best friend/freelance agency manager Bri, and, of course, my stoic Siamese cat, Wee. This book also would have not been possible if my amazing agent, Jean Sagendorph, hadn't sent me an email one day after finding me on TikTok. I never imagined this many people would want to know what I have to think about things. I still can't believe it some days, but I have to shout out God on that one.

I would lastly like to acknowledge my online haters, whom I have to thank for my fiery, determined, and passionately stubborn work ethic. Without your constant insults and accusations, I wouldn't be half of the force I am today.

To the many, many more books to come.

xoxo, the Freelance Fairy

FREELANCE YOUR WAY TO FREEDOM

1 You Can Be Financially Free

Man is born free, and everywhere he is in chains.

— Jean-Jacques Rousseau

If you ask anyone in your life what it means to have a stable job, they will tell you it's working at a 9-to-5 with a boss. We have been told this since we were in kindergarten when textbooks started to imply to us that success comes from an office job. We've all seen the illustrations that depict the person in the business suit with the briefcase, wearing the same three monochrome colors as they trudge their way into work. And from that moment on, it's that very concept of success that is pushed on us until we embody it ourselves. If we dare to veer off that path and do something different, we risk being ostracized from the people in our lives who believe that kind of risk is irresponsible.

As social creatures who thrive in communities, we're impacted by our peers. What they say and think about us matters. That's why philosopher Jean-Jacques Rousseau in *The Social Contract* explored why natural man who was free and happy living in the forest gave up autonomy for the modern condition of unhappiness, inequality, and dependency. He recognized that some benefits, like amenities and technology, come from leaving the forest, yet this trade-off makes people unhappier and more unequal than ever.

We are all born free, yet we line up for those invisible chains because we believe we must. That's where your journey into making the most of the remote work economy begins: the belief. The belief that you must work at the job, in the office building, with the boss, or else you are letting yourself and your family down. The belief that being a responsible adult means sacrificing part of yourself along the way. The belief that the only way to build real wealth is through giving up forty years of your life in a work space far away from your family.

These invisible chains are created inside our minds, which means they can be destroyed in the exact same place. You can—and deserve—to be financially free just as much as the next person. You don't need to prove yourself any more than you already have. You were born free, and to freedom you shall return through the basis of your own personal financial freedom.

Defining What Financial Freedom Means for You

Financial freedom is the status of being able to make decisions for the rest of your life without worrying about money. For some people, this can look like having $5 million in their bank account; for other people, it can be having a few hundred thousand dollars saved with no debt and 12 different side hustles that are expected to earn at least $500,000 each between now and that person's death.

Financial freedom can be tailored to everyone on the level of specifics. But one thing remains universal: it's the state in which you can do whatever you want with your life without worrying about money.

You must be thinking to yourself: "Yeah right, sounds too good to be true." That's because for 95% of people, it is too good to be true. And it's only too good because they continue to allow the invisible chains to keep them in one place, at one job, with one boss who doesn't respect them or their time. They perceive freedom to be too good to be true, so it remains too good. But for you, it's not too good at all—it's merely the bare minimum. Financial freedom is how you unlock the potential for the rest of your life and give yourself the opportunity to see what's out there, waiting for you.

We try to plan for our lives to the best of our ability, but we can't possibly plan for the abounding opportunities that can only come our way when we start to believe we are deserving of them. That's why the Law of Attraction could not be truer—we attract what we believe we deserve. We put out the energy into the world that we want to bounce right back to us. The most successful and wealthy people of our time today were not special or lucky; they were merely masters of their mindset and accepted the reality of financial freedom for themselves early on in their lives. They dropped their chains in pursuit of the unknown. And what they found is exactly what will be detailed in this book: accountability is the only sacrifice that must be made in the achievement of personal and financial independence.

Financial Freedom Is an Equal Opportunity Employer

Rousseau argued that when we left the forest to move into society, we created inequalities that never used to be there. Barriers to entry popped up in the form of status, education, skin color, and sex. In the forest, we could access any resources we needed to and there was no system to stop us. Yet, in society, we accept inequalities in the name of stability.

That's what makes the concept of financial freedom so incredible and surely something Rousseau would be praising if he were alive today. The pursuit of financial freedom is equally available to every single person in the world—hear me out. In the past, societal jobs in offices, government buildings, medical facilities, and law firms required individuals to obtain degrees. In order to obtain these degrees, people needed to receive primary education in a supportive setting that encouraged them to go to college. They would then need financial aid in order to go to higher education, where they were destined to graduate with insurmountable debt that made the idea of venturing into the unknown world of remote work too risky. This kind of system ostracizes individuals from lower socioeconomic communities and favors those with the money needed to access education and study materials.

In the world of financial independence, you don't need a college degree, a resume, or even a forward-facing photo of yourself. It doesn't matter what you look like or how old you are. Nothing about your past matters. You can get on anonymous freelancing marketplaces and learn skills for free on YouTube or TikTok. You can build a portfolio of free work you offer to do for friends and family when first starting out. You can set up affiliate marketing funnels and ecommerce landing pages that have nothing to do with you and your identity. You are truly, in every sense of the word, free.

Case Study: My Journey to Financial Freedom

I declared myself financially free in 2020 when I earned my millionth dollar on Fiverr. If that was all I had going at the time, I wouldn't have considered one million dollars to be enough to support me (age 27) for the rest of my life. But, with one million earned dollars that I intended to invest in multiple real estate investment properties, as well as six different side hustles at the time, including my online courses that average around $15,000 to $25,000 in passive sales per month, I declared myself financially free to my social media followers. If I were to stop working altogether and do nothing starting today, my freelance writing agency, which is now entirely managed by my best friend and virtual assistants, e-book sales, course sales, YouTube ads revenue, website ads revenue, investment property revenue, and TikTok/Instagram Reels revenue would comfortably support me for the rest of my life. I do not have to work another day if I do not want to.

The rest of this book is going to show you in detail how I was able to become financially free at 27 years old. We are going to look at the different side hustles, freelancing business structures, personal brands, and business tools that you can use in any combination to achieve financial freedom. And while we look at it, I want you to promise me that you are going to read over these pages believing that you deserve this kind of freedom, too.

Chapter 1 Key Points

- Any single person can make the choice to become financially free.
- Financial freedom does not have one blueprint definition; it is tailored per person.
- You must make the choice to take off your invisible chains.
- We attract what we believe we deserve.

I Freelancing

2 Why Freelancing First Makes Sense

Don't spend so much time trying to choose the perfect opportunity that you miss the right opportunity.

— Michael Dell

The concept of freelancers has been around for nearly 200 years, named for the free "lances" who were medieval mercenaries who would be paid to fight for a particular nation or person. These people didn't have a specific allegiance to any king or queen, but rather they traveled where the gold beckoned them. After they completed the war or battle for their payment, they were free to trudge on and find the next-highest bidder willing to pay for their temporary loyalty.

The modern-day freelancer is no different. And it's that very reason why you are going to grow your own freelancing brand first, before you conquer the pursuit of financial freedom.

What Is Freelancing?

A freelancer is an independent, self-employed person who is hired out on a per-project basis. Freelancers do not report to bosses, companies, or managers, and are responsible for supplying their own benefits. The trade-off is simple: a freelancer can make their own schedule, business, prices, and structure, in exchange for forgoing the health insurance, retirement, and other benefits that come from working a 9-to-5.

We will discuss in later chapters how this trade-off is incorrectly marketed, since freelancers can set up their own retirement accounts, buy health insurance, and benefit from tax credits and deductions that are not available to employed individuals.

Freelancers can run their businesses anywhere they want to—there are no rules. But it's most common for a freelancer to face the following decision when first starting out: Do I want to run my own business from a website, or do I want to use the big freelancing marketplaces like Fiverr and Upwork to grow my business? Technically, you can—and should—do both.

The fact that so much freedom is already awarded to you the moment you decide to start freelancing can be the very reason why so many people are scared to try it out. We are conditioned to work within rules and confines our entire adolescent and adult lives. We're told which classes we can and can't take. We're told what time to get to work, how to write emails according to the business guidelines, and how to report our Paid Time Off. We're told so many things that it's not uncommon to find yourself truly perplexed staring in the face of freelancing. With different structural options and no rules about what's right and wrong, how are you supposed to get started?

Believe me—I was there, too. I almost felt guilty, like I was doing something wrong working on my Fiverr freelance writing business back in 2016. I would look around in the Starbucks, wondering if someone was catching onto my "naughty" departure from society to write press releases and blogs in the corner. That is some deep psychological programming for you.

Fortunately, following the acceptance of remote work at the onset of the COVID-19 pandemic, freelancing became a popularly sought-after concept. Millions of people are quitting their jobs to take their current skill set they have developed at companies and go offer it to their own clientele. I applaud them for taking that initiative because not only will it pay off with the freedom for them to travel and see the world, but they will also enjoy higher overall earnings, considering that skilled freelancers earn more per hour than 70% of U.S. workers (Booth 2019).

Still, the concept of freelancing remains hard for people to understand, which is why I am going to show you just how simple it is to make it work for you. I believe freelancing first is the best way to pay down debt, get a feel for basic business practices like customer service and sales, and save up some extra cash you can use to open additional side hustles and investments down the line. Rome wasn't built in a day!

Case Study: My First Five Years of Freelancing

I started freelancing back in 2015 while I was still working at an office job. I sold one flat-rate editing gig on Fiverr for $5. I would edit anything, of any length, for that $5. And I didn't care that it was so cheap—it was still more money than I would have had without the gig.

The following year, after quitting my PR job, I began to freelance full time. I did nothing else but freelance until 2020. I wanted to devote every ounce of my energy and focus into understanding freelancing, my clients, and how to scale my business. I knew if I tried to do a zillion other things, I would miss valuable learning along the way. All the skills I learned freelancing solely became transferrable into everything else I do today. The skills you will learn freelancing are not just limited to that—they are skills that you can take with you for the rest of your life. The universality of these skills will make you fail proof in future economies.

Now, that is not to say that you must spend five years doing nothing but freelancing. There are so many freelancing resources available to you today that you can cut my timeline into a fraction—and I encourage you to do so! If you want to spend just one year freelancing before branching out, go for it. But before you do anything else, set up a freelancing empire that will carry you to that financial freedom finish line.

The Pros and Cons of Freelancing Marketplaces and Solo Businesses

Before we dive into the meat of freelancing, setting up a freelancing business, attracting clients, and making your money, let's break down the pros and cons of freelancing marketplaces like Fiverr versus solo businesses managed on your own website.

Freelancing Marketplaces

Pros

- **Built-in marketing departments:** Freelancing marketplaces use an algorithm to funnel you clients so you don't have to go out there and find them yourself.
- **Built-in dashboard tools:** Freelancing marketplaces sort orders chronologically for you, process payments, act as intermediaries in client disputes, and so forth.
- **Access to marketplace perks:** This can include discounted healthcare plans and packages, payment processors, and new features.
- **It costs no money to get started:** Since you give out 20% of your earnings to these platforms, they are free to use to start off.

Cons

- **Most take 20% of your earnings:** Freelancing marketplaces take a cut of your profits in exchange for funneling those clients.
- **Corporate overlording:** Freelancing marketplaces reserve the right to kick you off if you violate Terms of Service or anger the corporate overlords.
- **Profile anonymity:** Sites like Fiverr and Upwork require you to remain anonymous so you can't take clients off the platform.
- **Pay to play:** In recent years, sites like Fiverr have pushed $32/month seller mentoring programs that help you rank higher in search results.
- **There are timers on orders:** Once an order is placed, a timer starts ticking. You can change deadlines, but it's not great for your profile stats.

Solo Freelancing Businesses

Pros

- **You have total control over the business:** There are no rules or terms of service to violate—the business is unequivocally yours.

- **There is no anonymity:** You are front facing to your clients and create a much more meaningful and long-term relationship with them.

- **You can scale it into an agency easily:** The moment you have more work than you can handle, hire some virtual assistants to help you. Chapter 4 will go over this concept in depth.

- **You make your own schedule:** If something happens and you end up one day late on an order for a client, you are not going to be penalized the way you would on a freelancing marketplace.

Cons

- **You are responsible for everything:** You must be the customer service, sales, marketing, content, and payroll department, all rolled into one.

- **You must find your own leads:** No one is going to drop freelancing leads on your lap for free.

- **You must find your freelancing tools:** It's up to you to find invoicing/accounting software, chat software, and so forth when managing your business.

- **It costs money to start your own business:** A new website, URL, logo, LLC, and running ads can add up.

Which Option Is Better for You?

There is never a one-size-fits-all answer for anything in business. That's the beauty of it. But there is a general structure that you can follow on your quest to own a seven-figure agency.

First, start with the freelancing platforms. Think of these platforms as the bikes with training wheels. You lose autonomy and some money to them, but they provide you with safety nets. They alleviate the need for sales and placing ads, tracking funds and invoices, and strong-arming clients who don't pay. As a result, you can focus on the other elements of your business, like perfecting your pitches to your clients, adhering to client expectations, and creating perfect questionnaires that collect all the information you need from a client before an order begins.

While you spend your time focusing on these aspects, you will find that adding in the additional responsibilities down the line is manageable. You don't want to overwhelm yourself at first. Take your time with all of this and realize that in just a few months, using one or more freelancing platforms that were completely free to sign up on can change your life forever.

After you spend some time trading over your autonomy in exchange for the training wheels, you're going to get itchy. You're going to want some say in how your business runs, and you're especially going to want to be able to share your first name with your clients. That's when you're going to open your very own freelancing website off a platform.

Note: You can be on freelancing platforms *and* open your own freelancing website. There is no rule that says you cannot.

Just ensure your pricing is consistent between the two, so you do not confuse or upset your clients. Although your profiles are anonymous on many freelancing platforms, you will want to start collecting clients that you own directly through a freelancing website. We will go over how to do this in subsequent chapters.

When you open this website, it's going to take some time and require a new level of accountability from you. You're going to have to find a website designer to build the website (unless you want to take a stab at it). You're going to want to hire other freelancers (using the marketplaces is a great place to access freelancing talent for your own business) to make the logos, graphics, website content, and even use search engine optimization (SEO) for the entire thing. Then once that's all done, you're going to sit down and think about how you're going to find your clients. You have many options available to you, with the most popular being:

- Social media posting
- Social media groups (Facebook, Slack, and LinkedIn)
- Cold pitching
- Email marketing
- Virtual and in-person networking
- Advertisements

You will soon learn which methods you prefer for finding your leads. All of these can be done by virtual assistants for you, so you don't have to worry about it. We will review how to find, vet, and leverage virtual assistants in the forthcoming chapters.

Never Put All Your Eggs in One Basket

That is one of my all-time favorite sayings because it could not be truer in business. The volatility of working for yourself in freelancing is evident, no doubt. Yet you can crush that volatility into oblivion if you spread yourself out over multiple freelancing marketplaces and lead funnels. Who said you had to just pick one thing and cross your fingers? Although your employer has probably created a fear in you that you can't earn money to the side of your corporate job through their heinous "non-compete" requirements, with freelancing, you can compete against yourself repeatedly. In Chapter 3, we'll look at why you should get on multiple freelancing marketplaces when starting out.

Chapter 2 Key Points

- Freelancing can be tailored in any way that works for you.
- Start with freelancing platforms and work your way into your own solo freelancing business.
- Consider trying out multiple freelancing platforms when you are just getting started.
- Be sure never to put all your eggs in one basket.

3 Getting on More Than One Freelancing Platform

Never depend on a single income. Make investment to create a second source.

— Warren Buffett

The single biggest risk an adult takes today is the risk of relying on just one job, with one employer, for their sole income. As the COVID-19 pandemic proved rather quickly, no matter how long you've been with a firm, they can fire or furlough you, or worse, let you go for your beliefs. Sticking around hoping that one day your boss is going to notice how hard you've been working for decades isn't reliable any longer. And honestly, that's a good thing for you—you're free.

As humans, we are multi-dimensional creative beings with multiple interests. Elizabeth Gilbert put it best in her book *Big Magic*: "A creative life is an amplified life. It's a bigger life, a happier life, an expanded life, and a hell of a lot more interesting life. Living in this manner—continually and stubbornly bringing forth the jewels that are hidden within you—is a fine art, in and of itself" (Gilbert 2015, p. 12).

That's why you're going to get on more than one freelancing platform when starting out. There are countless different marketplaces available to you today, all with their pros and cons. Your preferences will be based on your personality, creativity, and the way in which you like to work with clients. Do you prefer shorter-timed projects that come and go? Fiverr makes more sense. Do you prefer longer-term projects that might require more interviewing in the beginning? Upwork is the place for you. But you can't know where you do—and don't—thrive until you've tried your hand at all the big marketplaces at your fingertips.

In the past, accessing these kinds of business havens cost money. The fact that you can try out all these different marketplaces, for free, seems to me like it should be illegal. I often feel that way today with all the free information just sitting online, waiting for us to access it. Never in history has it been this freely available, and I want every one of you to benefit from it!

That brings us to the question looming in your head: Which platforms should I try out? I am not endorsing any one of these platforms in this book. I am going to give you an impartial breakdown of the biggest platforms to consider, as well as a list of the other players in the game I have not personally experienced myself. As with anything in business, please always tread cautiously on any website where money is processed and use your best judgment.

The Big Three

Although there are plenty of up-and-coming freelancing marketplaces that stand to upset the current reigning three in the world of freelancing, these big three platforms are still the supreme brands at the time of writing. Let's look at a generic breakdown and the overall aims of each company.

Fiverr (Fiverr.com)

What started as a $5 freelancing platform has blossomed into its own freelancing universe equipped with Fiverr Business Accounts, online courses, Seller Plus programs, Fiverr PRO, and Fiverr Workspace. Sellers charge anything but $5 today, with most people starting at around $15–$25 per service they offer. Fiverr includes a ranking system of New Seller, Level 1, Level 2, and Top Level Seller, which helps sellers identify where they rank in the food chain on there. Each level has specific parameters the seller must satisfy before they advance to the next level. Many freelancers cap out at Level 2 seller and can still earn six figures per year without Top Level or Fiverr PRO accreditation.

As with most freelancing platforms, success on Fiverr is based on reviews. The more five-star reviews you have, the higher your profile will rank. Not to mention that these reviews double as social proof and assure your future clients you are going to do good work for them. But remember, Fiverr does take 20% of your earnings at all levels on the site, as well as a percentage of your tips that you receive. They also monitor correspondence and reserve the right to remove sellers that violate their Terms of Service.

Fiverr resonates best with freelancers who prefer:

- Fast-paced transactions that open and close quickly
- Not to engage in video calls with clients
- To work potentially part-time and limit the number of orders they take on weekly

I have personally used Fiverr the past seven years because I do not excel at the customer service side of freelancing and therefore do not want to be on calls or phone calls with clients. I believe my questionnaire is enough to ensure we have all necessary information presented for the order. I would rather work with short-term orders that come and go in volume, than hunker down with a few clients that have big budgets yet expect a lot of my attention. That is just my personal preference, since there is no one right way to do this.

Upwork (Upwork.com)

Whereas Fiverr launched in 2010 and enjoyed a jump on the market before Upwork solidified their name in 2015, the powerhouse freelancing marketplace was quickly able to give Fiverr a run for its money. Positioning themselves as a more "upscale" place to find clients, Upwork became known as the more affluent freelancing marketplace at the time. When Fiverr was indeed offering $5 services, they were getting lots of clients, sure, but they weren't quality clients. The clients that wanted quality work with bigger budgets went to Upwork. Since Fiverr has moved far away from $5 with its top 1% of the platform program, Fiverr PRO, today, this isn't exactly the case at present—yet many would argue that those with bigger budgets still prefer to use Upwork.

Upwork is structured differently from Fiverr. It's an open marketplace, but clients require freelancers to do some interviews, sample test orders, and so forth before deciding to use them. The freelancers consent because many times, the projects include multimonth requirements with lucrative pay. Upwork does also reduce its 20% fee to 10% if the order payment amount goes above $500.

Besides that, Upwork offers the same benefits as Fiverr, working as intermediaries in payment disputes, offering workflow organization and invoicing support, and other tools that improve the overall freelancing business.

Upwork resonates best with freelancers who prefer:

- Slower-paced transactions and more personal client interaction
- Longer-term-minded people who would rather have one to two clients as opposed to 20 in one week
- Higher-quality clients with bigger budgets

I tried out Upwork for about six months back when I was first starting out. I quickly learned I do not care for the customer service side of things (as much as I should), and therefore did not like all the interviewing and sample orders I had to complete. Discovering this about myself was critical in my growth as a freelancer, which would never have happened if I had not tried out a bunch of different sites in the beginning.

LinkedIn (LinkedIn.com)

LinkedIn has always been somewhat of a freelancing networking platform, but it really stepped forward with an intent to battle it out with Fiverr and Upwork when it launched its LinkedIn Services Marketplace. Set up to function like any ol' freelancing marketplace, LinkedIn is diving into the hundreds of millions of people who use the freelancing platform to offer services not traditionally popular on Fiverr or Upwork: executive coaching and software development. With droves of ex-corporateers on LinkedIn who have plenty of executive coaching and software experience, LinkedIn is setting themselves up to have the "highest quality clients in the market" for freelancers on the site.

Since LinkedIn enjoys such a huge share of the online market, they aren't exactly rushing to provide all the nice tools and support that you can find on the other two websites. But just using your LinkedIn Direct Messages, alone, can be the answer to scaling a freelancing business that you own 100%. Hire virtual assistants to answer the messages for you, as well as send out sales pitches to clients who could be potential fits for your business.

Better yet, there are plenty of automation software options that will send out the LinkedIn messages indefinitely while your virtual assistants answer the people who reply to the messages. All of this can be done without ever having to lift a finger.

I believe LinkedIn's power in the world of freelancing is going to continue to grow. Their numbers tower over those of Fiverr and Upwork, and if they can build in any semblance of freelancer-supportive tools, they could emerge the obvious winners in this battle. Therefore, spend some time sprucing up your LinkedIn profile and setting up your LinkedIn Service Page.

Where Else Can You Freelance?

Your freelancing potential is not—and should not—be limited to just these three platforms. The opportunities continue to increase with more and more competition and plenty of backing from venture capital seeping its way into the world of freelancing (probably because they know remote work is going to be the dominant form of work in the years to come).

Here is a general list of other freelancing platforms, in no particular order, for you to consider (proceed with caution always):

- **Contra** (Contra.com): The first 0% independent work platform that focuses on networking and community tools for freelancers.

- **Legiit** (Legiit.com): Modeled after Fiverr in nature, Legiit aims to be an open marketplace that is more fluid and boasts higher-quality clients.

- **Freelancer** (Freelancer.com): This one has been around for a while and is a generic marketplace. There are some scams on there, so use your best judgment.

- **Toptal** (Toptal.com): This marketplace distinguishes itself as one where software engineers, finance experts, and product managers abound.

- **Guru** (Guru.com): With a general lower fee of 8.95% that it takes from the freelancer, Guru is quickly becoming a fan favorite in recent months.

- **Designhill** (Designhill.com): For graphic designers only, Designhill has 227,000 designers and counting, with plenty of room for new freelancers.

- **Dribbble** (Dribbble.com): This marketplace for graphic designers is an all-in-one design portfolio platform, jobs, and recruiting site.

- **We Work Remotely** (Weworkremotely.com): This remote work marketplace focuses specifically on remote work jobs that can be part-time, freelance, or full-time in nature.

- **Slack** (Slack.com): You can join different freelancing channels in Slack where jobs are posted and apply right inside the app.

- **Facebook groups** (Facebook.com/groups): Don't discount the power of joining freelancing Facebook groups and looking for posted jobs every day.

Every single one of these options is free to try out. Give yourself a one- or two-month grace period to see if you like the way the platforms work. You will find in that time the best platforms for you will become apparent. Starting out on two or three solid platforms is a guaranteed way to ensure your freelancing business is going to be successful moving forward. All the tips I am going to share with you about optimizing those profiles and landing good-paying jobs can be applied to every single one of these platforms. Not to mention that since they are all in fierce competition with one another, they are rolling out new features daily that do nothing but benefit you.

It's time to master the art of positioning yourself on a freelancing marketplace in a way that distinguishes you from the competition. Let's look at your overall branding, imagery, and wording. The number one thing in the back of your mind on any one of these sites should be communicating trust to the client as directly as possible. The sooner they trust you, the sooner they are going to do business with you.

Chapter 3 Key Points

- Get on more than one freelancing platform when starting out.
- Strongly consider checking out the Big Three: LinkedIn, Fiverr, and Upwork.

- Recognize that you are a multidimensional person and may thrive on certain marketplaces while losing interest in others.

- Aim to establish your freelancing business on at least two freelancing platforms moving forward.

4 Why You Should Create a Freelancing Agency

If you don't build your dream, someone will hire you to help build theirs.

— Tony Gaskins

When I first started freelancing on Fiverr, I was beyond content with my business embedded right inside of the platform. I was free to move around wherever I wanted to, I could take naps in the middle of the "workday" if I didn't feel well, and I was making more than any corporate job was ever going to pay me. I was happy as sh*t.

As time wore on, I started to experience the typical yearning for something more with my business. Any freelancer or entrepreneur will agree—it's always about the journey, never the destination. I am no different. My Fiverr business was booming, I had no debt, and I felt pretty freaking grateful that I made that irresponsible decision to quit my job at only 22 years old. Yet, my mind wondered: Could I replicate this process . . . again? Is there more I could be doing? Had I conquered the first step of building a freelancing empire?

I started to explore the concept of taking my Fiverr momentum and turning it into my own business—something that was unequivocally mine. The entire purpose of freelancing in the first place is to be your own boss. We all want autonomy and control over our income. That's why the trade-off on freelancing platforms inspires almost all freelancers to venture off (on a timeline that works for them) and turn the entire thing into a fully established business.

I began to explore freelancing without a platform. It felt as though I were taking those training wheels off my bicycle finally, seeing if I could balance all on my own. Freelancing clients I accumulated off anonymous freelancing sites were all mine—no one could do anything about it. That kind of wild freedom is truly addicting—it's a feeling I want all of you to know and enjoy. It's the opposite manifestation of feeling helpless at the feet of a boss who could, at any moment, decide to send you packing. It's the definition of total and unadulterated job security.

First, let's look at what a freelancing agency is, and how they are typically structured.

What Is a Freelancing Agency?

A freelancing agency is defined as a freelancing business structure in which additional freelancers do work for you, the original freelancer. Sounds like *Inception,* right? These are freelancers who work on your client projects, below you, while you manage the flow of work, proofing it before delivering the finished product to the paying customer.

Freelancing agencies come in many shapes and sizes, starting with just a few freelancers below you, up through thousand-person operations that span the globe. For the purposes of this book, we're going to stick with the 1-to-10-person basic model.

Freelancing agencies, in essence, are designed to shift the burden of completing every single order a client requests onto the freelancers below you. However, that doesn't mean you're absolved of all work demands and requirements—it merely shifts those demands. As the owner of a freelancing agency, you will shift into a management role that requires more customer service, work allocation, marketing, and sales. Of course, every agency is structured differently, to the preference of the founding freelancer. And with virtual assistants, you can pick and choose which agency services you want to oversee daily. None of this is ever a one-size-fits-all structure.

When and How Do You Start a Freelancing Agency?

At some point in your freelancing journey, you are going to want to own your own agency. Believe me. When this point comes, you might be asking yourself: "Okay, now what? How do I start an agency?"

First, do not feel the pressure to start a freelancing agency your first or second year in business. You will notice, however, naturally, that you want to explore starting your own agency as time wears on. The beauty of freelancing is working without a ceiling. The limit does not exist. It's something that can be shocking to us, coming from a workforce in which everything we do is capped. When you hit that point of wanting your own agency, you'll know which chapter to open in this book.

Here is the general overview of how an agency comes to fruition:

- **Step 1:** Determine the services your agency is going to offer. You want to niche down in this instance. Why? The niche tells customers that you are specialized in a particular topic. They will quickly trust you as an "expert."

- **Step 2:** Choose the location you are going to use for the agency headquarters. Since most freelancing agencies are entirely virtual, this is not an incredibly important detail. But, for taxation purposes, you may want to headquarter the business in a state (or country) that includes extra tax breaks and benefits.

- **Step 3:** Name the agency. Think of something fun, memorable, and zany. People hire freelancers when they want to get away from the stuffiness of corporate culture. They don't want to stumble on a freelancing agency's name that could double for a corporate commercial building label. Be sure to pick a name that has an available URL. For example, the name "Freelance Writer" probably does not have freelancewriter.com available for purchase (if it does, it most likely costs thousands of dollars). Get creative and check sites like GoDaddy.com to review if the URL is available or not.

- **Step 4:** Structure the agency. I recommend starting small in the beginning. When I started building out my agency, for many years it was just myself with one writer below me. I have expanded it to include six writers, two virtual assistants, and one personal agency assistant who manages the entire operation for me if I am spending the day recording a podcast or a YouTube video. Types of freelancers to consider adding to an agency include general workload managers, technical co-founders, partners or CEOs, accountants, lawyers, freelancers, and virtual assistants.

- **Step 5:** Start hiring. Finding quality talent to join your agency is key. Freelancing is first and foremost based on quality services. Prior education doesn't matter, nor does industry standing. Clients want excellent projects delivered to them time and time again. Don't settle for lackluster talent—your ideal freelancers are out there. You can find many of them on social media, looking for additional work.

- **Step 6:** Set up a payment structure. It's typical to pay your freelancers based on word count, or size of project delivered. You can also opt for an hourly structure if that makes more sense. Pay the freelancers biweekly while tracking the work that they do. You can also ask them to track their own payroll and submit it to you biweekly to crosscheck with yours (this is what I do). For revisions, set the parameters so the freelancers are clear on compensation. You may opt to compensate a certain amount for revisions that take 15 minutes or less, versus hour-long revisions or complete overhaul of deliveries.

- **Step 7:** Register the business (I personally registered mine as an LLC). Using the EIN (Employer Identification Number, which you get from the IRS), open a business bank account where you will process all the money that is made through the business. Not only is this a legally sound thing to do, but you can also claim additional tax deductions and increase your tax savings by using a business bank account. Your accountant will thank you.

- **Step 8:** Collect your clients. Once the general framework for the agency is created, you can push out your services in a variety of marketing avenues, like social media content, social media ads, Facebook groups, Discord groups, Reddit or Quora threads, email marketing, and so forth (we will go over marketing in more depth in Part 3 of this book). You want to find long-term returning clients that plan to work with you for months at a time. It saves you money if you don't have to onboard a new client every single day for a project that is only going to take one or two hours.

- **Step 9:** Draft proposal templates, questionnaires, and contracts. When you manage an agency without a freelancing platform, it's on you to manage the flow of services and money. Clients will typically request a proposal from you before agreeing to the contract. Proposals can take a long time to write, so use your best judgment if you feel it's a client that's going to stick around for a while. Your questionnaire should model the one you already have inside of your Fiverr or Upwork account. Contracts should lay out the general details of the start and end date, deliverables, pricing structure, and revision policy. Consulting an attorney when creating your contract draft is advised.

Case Study: How I Find My Personal Freelancing Leads

I love to partner with PR firms that want to outsource the bulk of their writing to my team. It minimizes the number of people I need to message if 50% of my work comes from just one person. In order to find these clients, I use a mixture of email marketing and social media posting. I have my VAs work with my email automation specialist to create leads lists, email sequences, and follow-ups. I then have my personal assistant take the calls with potential clients and onboard them into our agency.

While they do all of that for me, I spend half of my days creating content on social media. This not only gets me brand deals and sponsorships, but it also gets my name out there so PR firms can find me without my ever having to pay for an advertisement.

To date, I have not spent a single cent on marketing or advertising my freelancing business. And you don't have to, either.

Case Study: My Freelancing Agency, Alex Fasulo LLC

I have proudly not spent a single cent on advertising my freelancing business since getting started years ago. I rely solely on social media content, marketing, and social media groups to get the word out there about my agency. Once you start collecting emails, it will grow itself without your intervention.

Today, I work with both part-time and full-time freelancers. I also look for individuals specializing in different topics so I can offer a range of expertise to my clients. Managing the agency takes work at times, but it's worth it to go to sleep at night and know that you own the access to every single one of your clients. Relying on other companies isn't an end-all, be-all solution.

Beyond the agencies, freelancing profiles, and opportunities comes the number one reason you want to make this work: the lifestyle. Typing away on your laptop from an Airbnb outside of Joshua Tree or at a café in Paris is one reason the freelancing lifestyle is so sought after. Position yourself for the kind of freelancing lifestyle that meets your wants and needs. Yes, you can finally consider your *wants* in the world of freelancing. The next chapter explains how to embrace this new kind of living.

Chapter 4 Key Points

- Freelancing agencies are the logical next step after freelancing platforms.
- Setting up an agency can be hard work, but the overall structure of the business will relieve you of daily freelancing tasks for clients.
- Owning an agency will challenge you to learn new skills like customer service management and work allocation.
- Nothing compares to 100% owning every single one of your clients in your business.

5 Adjusting to a Freelancing Lifestyle

Success is a sum of small efforts—repeated day in and day out.

— Robert Collier

And now for the fun part: the freelancing lifestyle. It's why all, or probably most of you, want to make this a reality for yourself. Hell, it's why I quit my job with absolutely zero plan. What's the point of living if we don't have some control over our lifestyle? People are tired of being forced into the same 40-hour workweek structure. Can you blame them?

Once you become accustomed to a freelancing lifestyle, you will never be able to go back to any other lifestyle, I am sorry to inform you. It's an infection that has no cure. You've been warned!

At the very basis of the freelancing lifestyle is a new accountability in which you, and solely you, are responsible for waking up and meeting client deadlines. This will probably be the biggest deviation from your previous 9-to-5. No one is going to yell at you if you don't come into the office by 9 a.m. No one is going to monitor how long you take to get your coffee from Dunkin' Donuts. And no one is calculating your Paid Time Off to see if you still have time for a vacation at the end of the year. All of it evaporates.

But there is an exchange for pure freedom that goes on. It means that the buck stops with you. You're the one who must map out what time you need to wake up and how many hours a project is going to take. It's you who needs to adhere to any timeline a client might establish. It's you who needs to make sure you don't deliver late on a Fiverr order, which, if it becomes a habit, can sink your profile rather quickly.

Accountability starts and ends with you as a freelancer. This can be scary to people at first. We've spent our entire lives being told what to do, where to go, and what time to show up. We go on autopilot and don't realize that we've completely ceded our happiness and time to someone else. When we finally get that kind of control over our time back, we might panic. And if you do panic, don't worry—you are not alone. That's why anticipating this kind of shock as you foray into a freelancing lifestyle is the best thing you could do to set yourself up for freedom.

So, what does a "freelancing lifestyle" look like? What should you expect?

What Is a Freelancing Lifestyle?

A freelancing lifestyle is living differently day-to-day in order to meet the demands and expectations of your clientele. Some days, it might mean waking up at 7 a.m. to catch a Zoom call with your client who lives 12 hours ahead of you. Other days, it might mean being able to sleep in until 10 a.m. since you only have one project due by the evening. In essence, there is no structure to a freelancing lifestyle—it's however you want to outline it.

You have total control over your schedule as a freelancer. You can stack work on Mondays and Tuesdays, taking Wednesdays off every week. You can move work around so you are able to sleep in every day, or you can wake up early and have all your work done by lunchtime so you can go golf and sip on martinis until dinnertime. You can even live in a van and travel the country, syncing up project deliveries when you have WiFi at McDonalds or Starbucks. (I know people who follow these different schedules.) There is no one right way to live as a freelancer.

As the sole responsible person for your freelancing business and schedule, if you fall short, deliver late, or forget about a client, that accountability falls on you. It can't be pushed off to a boss or a manager. There is no middleman to jump in and protect you from the wrath of an angry client. You face the brunt of it. Now, that might sound scary, like more responsibility than you want to shoulder, but hear me out. Forcing yourself into this kind of accountability will teach you more about business, life, making money, and happiness than anything else will. You will become the kind of professional who can thrive in any industry moving forward. Facing the accountability head-on will make you proud of yourself. It will give you a feeling of elation we have been robbed of by being thrust into corporate jungles. There's something *so human* about it.

And the thing is, you are going to fall short at times. I know I have as a freelancer! You are not perfect, and you are never going to be perfect. It's humbling to fall short with a client and have them remind you directly what you did wrong. The middleman coddles us in corporations, keeping us protected from the big, bad clients that loom on the other side of your Microsoft software. Working with clients directly will teach you about communication, customer service, and emotional intelligence (EI). Increasing your EI will make you a more effective, enjoyable, and respected person in everything you do in your life. Considering that EI has been declining among the population over the past two decades (Ellwood 2021), refining your personal ability to recognize and process others' emotions will make you that much more empowered in the world of business.

Structuring a Productive Freelancing Lifestyle

Now I don't want you to jump into the world of freelancing with zero plan for how you are going to structure your time or workload. You can customize it however you prefer, but I am going to provide you with some suggestions to ensure you are as successful as possible right from the get-go.

- **Step 1:** Identify your productive periods. Every person varies—some people are alert in the wee hours of the morning; others prefer to power up in the evening when everyone else is asleep. It doesn't matter when your A game occurs; it just matters that you know when that time is. If you don't know when you are your most focused, practice the next 24 hours doing freelancing-related tasks. See which time intervals make you sleepier, or which ones encourage you to procrastinate. Note: if you have ADHD or any other neurodivergent diagnosis, your periods of focus shift daily. Still, freelancing can work better for this kind of thinking when compared to a typical 9-to-5.

- **Step 2:** Identify your attention drains. Are you someone who can't go more than five minutes without checking your Instagram? If so, consider turning off the notifications on your phone, or putting your phone in another room while you enter your working flow state. If you're like me, you can't work while other people talk around you (writer probs). I identified this early and have created silent spaces where I can get my important work done.

- **Step 3:** Sleep, hydrate, and prioritize your focus. In a lot of ways, your mind needs to be sharper and more alert if you are going to work for yourself. No one can step in and pick up the slack. You need to "biohack" your way to the highest level of focus possible (believe me). This means that going on a bender until 4 a.m. and waking up violently hung over isn't going to go well with freelancing. I personally cannot do any sort of writing if I am hung over. I also cannot focus on work after lunch if I eat a large amount of food, particularly carbs. I therefore prioritize proteins, veggies, and fruit during my focus time. I also avoid drinking in the evening if I know I have a lot of freelancing to do the next day. Feed your brain with foods, water, exercise, and rest so that it can operate to its full potential. People often fail to mention how important it is to take care of your body if you want to work for yourself!

- **Step 4:** Find other people in a freelancing lifestyle. I am not telling you to ditch all your corporate friends. But it is incredibly important that you find new people in your life living this same kind of lifestyle. They will be your rocks when you are feeling stressed or overwhelmed. And it's easy to find these people—they are on social media, clearly labeled as freelancers, looking for people like you to bond with. Find a few of these people to be there for you as you slip into this new lifestyle. This is especially important if your family, significant other, and/or best friend are not supportive of your new decision.

- **Step 5:** Learn to love content batching. This is probably my favorite time management hack of all time. Content batching is when you have a certain task that you need to do every day, and you do all of it for the week in one two-hour window. I do this with recording TikToks, podcasts, YouTubes, and writing blogs for my website. If you need to check over payroll, for example, every day of the week, carve out a time on Saturday when you do the entire weeks' worth of payroll at once. Batching is how you will be able to open holes in your week, like entire days off or afternoons off. If you make yourself do the same 13 things every single day, you are going to feel as though you are back in a corporate job. Play around with your time blocks!

- **Step 6:** Make time for noncompensated hobbies. A funny thing happens when you start working for yourself—you start to see the monetary potential in everything around you. You start to realize that truly anything can be turned into a business. Starting with your freelancing business, you may want to start making content on social media, accruing sponsorships, and posting affiliate links to your website. I encourage all of that, but I also implore you to keep some hobbies and time for yourself. You need to have hobbies you can turn to if you are feeling overloaded. For me, that's taking photos, going on drives, working out, reading books, cooking (barely, I am a horrible cook), going to the beach, or learning additional new hobbies (currently trying to learn how to play golf, and completely unrelatedly, also DJ).

If you follow all six of these steps, you will be more than prepared to venture out into a world in which you are your own boss. Once you get your structure all set up, you will realize there are really no cons to be in total control of your time. You can finally see family that lives halfway around the world; you can be with sick loved ones if they need your attention at the hospital; you can manage your own sicknesses or auto immune diseases with less pressure at home; you can travel anywhere you want; and you can choose to stay home with your children while they grow up. Most importantly, you can finally feel a sense of control over your life again.

Case Study: My Personal Freelancing Work Structure

Although no two days are ever the same for me, I do try to follow a similar routine weekly. I do believe some element of predictable routine is conducive to success. We are creatures of habit after all. I am my most focused, by far, in the morning. Therefore, I stack my "hardest work" of the day before noon. Here is what a typical Monday might look like for me:

- 6:30 a.m.: I wake up and check my email inbox.
- 7:00 a.m.: I get up and put my workout clothes on.
- 7:15–8 a.m.: I go on a walk and typically listen to a podcast (right now I am binging Joel Osteen—it's incredibly positive and gets me feeling good for the day). I try to walk 10,000 steps every day if possible.

- 8–11 a.m.: I sit down at my laptop and crunch out my hardest freelancing work of the day. This can include writing, answering emails, making graphics, and conferencing with my team.

- 11:00 a.m.: I usually break to either stretch or do a little weighted exercise.

- 11:30 a.m.: I start my social media posting for the day, usually by posting a TikTok.

- 12:00 p.m.: I break to eat some lunch and relax for an hour or so.

- 1–3 p.m.: This is normally my content recording window for social media videos, podcasts, and so forth.

- 3–4 p.m.: I post to Instagram and other social media channels, checking in on stats.

- 4–5 p.m.: I may record influencer and sponsorship content here for paying clients. I may also do more freelancing work.

- 5–6 p.m.: I check in with my general agency manager to see how everything is running.

- 6:30 p.m.: I try to shut down for the day. I am not good at it—I still end up checking emails and social media until 9 p.m. or so.

- 9:00 p.m.: I try to read every single day, either business books or the Bible. Reading is so important.

- 11:00 p.m.: I try to power down to go to sleep—I'm not always successful at this.

If I am traveling, for example, then I want to be able to break by 11 a.m. and enjoy the rest of my day. In this case, I will stack my work up the week before to clear it so I can spend my time exploring. I typically still work a few hours in the morning, even on trips. But I know people who totally unplug for weeks or months at a time (look at Tim Ferriss from *The 4-Hour Workweek*) and make it work.

This is a routine that I have slowly created for myself after years of learning when I am most technically focused versus creatively focused. My brain can handle intense technical work much more efficiently at 9 a.m. than it can at 3 p.m. Yet at 3 p.m., I feel my most creative to record social media content and come up with new podcast topics. I was only able to identify this from trial and error. You will know your focus periods impeccably, too, after doing this for a few weeks.

Don't fear the unpredictability of a freelancing lifestyle. It's the unpredictability that makes it so exciting and invigorating. You won't wake up on Monday, loathing your time ahead that day. Instead, you will be curious to find out what awaits you and your business.

In order to have a successful freelancing business that you carry with you day after day, you need to have happy, paying customers. The best way to keep them coming back for more is to refine your customer service skills. In Chapter 6, we go over some customer service hacks that will help you scale a successful business.

Chapter 5 Key Points

- A freelancing lifestyle revolves around personal accountability.
- Although you have more freedom than ever before, it is on you to create a schedule in which you can be your most productive for clients.
- Spend time learning about your focus periods and when you are your most alert.
- No two freelancing schedules are the same—create one that works for you and your goals.

6 Meeting Customer Expectations

The customer is always right.

— Harry Gordon Selfridge

Do I believe the customer is always right? Absolutely not. But that quote holds weight to it, whether you agree with ole Harry or not.

Your entire freelancing business is based upon paying customers. Without them, you have no business. You can't exist without them. So even when they are making you want to throw your laptop out the window (been there), you must realize it's ultimately your responsibility as the freelancer to minimize all miscommunications, confusions, and lack of information.

When I was first starting out freelancing, I was young and immature. Clients would occasionally tell me they hated my work, and I would fire back at them—quickly. Instead of listening to their feedback, I would take it personally and say things on Fiverr that got me account warnings. Yes, I am not immune to account warnings—I am just like everyone else.

Over time, I learned that it's in my best interest to work with these people. They are the ones handing over the money at the end of the day. Instead of taking their dissatisfaction personally, I started to upgrade my business in a way that anticipated their complaints. When one client would say the blog was missing X, I would go into the blog questionnaire and add X to it. That way, the next customer wouldn't complain about X—I was proactive in fixing it.

Customers can guide your freelancing business in a better direction than you could ever take it. Listening to what they have to say and doing your best to work with it results in a win-win: you will make more money, have a higher number of customers that return, and learn about what parts of your business aren't set up correctly.

When I had this epiphany, I realized that the customer, in a way, *is* always right.

The Top Three Freelancing Customer Expectations

Customers are going to expect a lot from you as the freelancer. They are entrusting you to get their work done in a timely and quality manner. They believe you are the most qualified person for the job, given their time constraints and what they need done. The more quickly you assure them that they did, indeed, pick the right person, the more likely they will become a returning customer. And the more returning freelancing customers you have, the more quickly your business will scale: 65% of my freelancing business is based on customers that come back for more.

When customers show up at your virtual doorsteps, what are they going to expect from you? How can you prepare to meet expectations you don't necessarily even know yet? Here are the top three freelancing customer expectations to prepare for:

1. **A complete information collection process.** Customers are going to assume you know how to collect the information you need to do their order. They are not going to assume that you may be still working on your process and don't necessarily know how to get that information yet. Many times, the biggest freelancing miscommunications can occur when a freelancer does not get all the information they need to do the order in X amount of time. The number one way to ensure this process is as smooth as possible is to create a questionnaire that is thorough and requires mandatory responses. Your questionnaire should have at least 10 questions in it, requesting everything from the client's business name and location to their website, prior work done for them, and what they want done in this order. If a client feels the questionnaire is too long or extensive for them to fill out, you will dodge a bullet. You want to work with clients that take you and your work seriously.

2. **A clear revision policy.** Customers will take advantage of your revision policy if you are not upfront and clear about it from the start. I clearly tell my clients that two revisions are included as part of the price. A third revision will need to be compensated based on the extent of its request. So long as I tell them this before the order starts, they have no problem agreeing to it. It's when you tell them this information after the first draft has been delivered that they get upset. They feel that you are changing the rules or withholding information from them. It's better to be straightforward and transparent before the order starts, than apologetic and be timid after there's a communication breakdown.

3. **Honesty about the status and completion of the order.**
Customers want you to check in with them. You may have
15 clients on your end, but they only have you, their sole
freelancer, on their mind. After a day or two, they want to
know that you are alive and working on their order without
any issues. If you deliver only a partial order because you felt
some piece of information was missing, they are going to
wonder why you didn't ask them days ago. That's why
procrastinating with orders doesn't fly in the world of
freelancing—clients want to think you spent slow,
methodical time getting their work done (even if this wasn't
the case). Upon every order submission, it's wise to look it
over for any informational holes before you wait another few
days to actually get started. Don't be shy in keeping your
client updated. Even if you check in to say, "Hello there! I
am working hard at completing this order for you. I will be
in touch with any questions." That's enough to keep them
calm and trusting.

How to Set the Right Freelancing Tone

Often, my order cancelations wouldn't come around for poor
order deliveries; they would come around due to lack of
communication. People think with their emotions, whether they
realize it or not.

Since people think with their emotions, setting the right
tone with them is imperative. You could deliver the most
beautiful ebook in the entire world, but with poor customer
service and manners, still end up with a three-star review. That's
why you want to give yourself the best chance at getting a
five-star review and a tip. It starts with how you establish the
initial client relationship.

When a client first messages you or reaches out to you about your services, they are looking for you to communicate some sense of authority and confidence. They want to know that you are an expert and are going to handle everything from A to Z for them. If they sense you are a pushover, shy, or unsure of yourself, they are going to take advantage—or possibly not book your services.

Establishing a positive, polite, yet authoritative tone is the best way to ensure a happy customer. This means you are going to be kind, responsive, and respectful, while also clearly establishing what you will, and will not, be offering with the service. It's just as important to make the client aware of what they *will not* be receiving, as it is to go over what they get with your service. This makes you seem transparent and again, effectively avoids any miscommunications down the line. You should also communicate your revision policy at this time to the client as well.

Now, you may be thinking: Won't speaking so "aggressively" to the client turn them off? I find that the more direct I am with clients, the more they respect me. In a way, they love it. They love thinking you are going to control the entire process so they can sit back, relax, and enjoy the ride. For the longest time, I thought I had to be gentle and delicate with clients to keep them happy. Boy, was I wrong! I come right out and state everything at face value to them—and they love it.

Here are some sample messages that can be used with clients to set initial expectations:

- "Hi there! I am so happy you are considering working with me. I have X experience in this field and would love nothing more than to bring your brand to life. With my service, I offer ABC. I do not offer XYZ currently. My revision policy includes two revisions. All additional revisions will need to be compensated based on the time demand. I look forward to working together."

- "I can't wait to get to work. With my service, I offer ABC. I do not offer XYZ currently. Please let me know you are aware of the services that will, and will not, be offered. If this is satisfactory to you, I would love to proceed. My revision policy includes two free revisions, with all additional revisions compensated according to time demands. Let's get to work!"

Always include some element of enthusiasm for bringing their dreams to life. Customers are inherently selfish and want to know that you are passionate about advancing their brand. They want to think that in some way, you believe in their vision. You don't have to agree with them or their brand at all. But remember: business is business. The more quickly you remove your personal offense and feelings from the transaction, the more quickly you are going to scale your business. I am not saying there is no place for emotions in business—but there is no place to take personal offense to requests of the client.

Little Gestures to Keep Customers Happy

As I mentioned earlier, customers are inherently selfish. They are using your services to advance their brand. However, it's a fair transaction because they are paying you for your time. But they are not paying you to know more about you—they are paying you to provide your expertise in advancing their specific project. Therefore, the more excited you act about their project, the more they are going to like you.

Little gestures complimenting the client or commenting on their product/service can be the difference in reviews, tips, and returning clients. If your client is selling the world's first solar-powered cat food dispensary product, letting them know their idea is "great" and "genius" when you deliver their order can go a long way. Or, letting them know that you believe their product is going to be successful and/or helpful for cat owners can still tickle their fancy.

I used to deliver orders very robotically, simply stating, "Here is your delivery. Thanks for the gig! Let me know if you want any changes made." It was a fine response to send, but it wasn't great. It didn't get my clients enamored with me and my services. It was very cut and dry. They want to feel that everything has been customized for them—and them alone. I should have delivered the order stating, "Wow, as a crazy cat lady, I would buy this product instantly for my cat. I had so much fun writing this for you. Let me know if you need any revisions made. Cheers!"

See how much more personal, fun, and positive that response is? Tone can go a long way with these people, especially in a world where we are only communicating with text-written responses. Since I don't permit video calls for potential clients (I do not feel video conferencing helps a writer understand a written project at all—I would much rather receive instruction in writing), written communication is all we have. Don't be afraid to throw in some exclamation points and emojis to humanize yourself with the client.

For freelancers who do have to engage video calls for their business, be sure to outline the exact time allotted for the call with the client ahead of time. This implies a certain level of authority from you and ensures you are not giving one client considerably more time than the others. Send your questionnaire to the client ahead of time and request that they fill it out before the call. That way, you can dive right into the nuts and bolts of the project, saving time for both of you as well as miscommunications. Many freelancers will record their client calls using software like Zoom so they can refer back to them.

One of the best lesser-known side effects of freelancing is the fact that you will become friends with some of these people. I have been working with some clients for seven years. I know more about them than I do about a lot of my extended family. Some of my clients send me Christmas cards and photos when their kids are born. We follow each other on social media and plan to even visit each other if we ever end up in the same location. This results from being kind, open, transparent, and excited with the client. They're a human just like you—it's your responsibility as the freelancer to set the right tone.

Dealing with Unhappy or Downright Irrational Clients

It's going to happen. You're going to log onto your computer one day, open Fiverr or your email, and see a scathing message from a client. You spent hours the day before perfecting their order for them, and this message makes your heart sink. You feel like crap because you don't understand (1) why they are so mad at you and (2) how they couldn't love the work you did for them.

The first time this happens to everyone hurts. I am not going to lie and tell you that it doesn't! It's almost a rite of passage in a way, because statistically, if you work with 50 people, at least one of them is going to be a downright a**hole.

You can't avoid it. Just know that when it happens to you, it doesn't mean you are an "imposter" or that you are bad at your craft; it just means you've worked with enough people to stumble on that bad one.

When this happened to me during my first few years freelancing, I was devastated. Back then, there weren't resources, YouTube videos, or Facebook groups I could join to vent (therefore, I opened my Facebook group "Freelancing Mentorship with Alexandra Fasulo"! I don't want anyone to feel alone enduring this). I had to suck it up the old-fashioned way, swallow my pride, and keep moving forward. I didn't know how to deal with unhappy clients effectively at all—I would take it personally, fire back at them, get one-star reviews, or cancel the orders. It was rough.

Fast forward a few years, and I have developed a few techniques for dealing with completely unhinged people. The first step is to anticipate that it is going to happen. If you approach freelancing hoping that you're never going to encounter angry clients, you are going to be shocked when it does happen to you and totally ill prepared. The second step is to have a plan in place when it does happen, so you can salvage what's possible during the blowup.

Here are some of my techniques that keep me from telling angry clients what I really think of them:

- **Presaved responses.** These are going to save your life. In Fiverr, you can save presaved responses that you click on and use whenever you want. It's not only a great time-saving tool, but it's also a great mental health tool as well. When all you want to do is respond back, "Yeah, well, you can F off" to a client, click on the presaved response instead and go for a walk. This response should look something like, "I am so sorry you feel this way. I have worked very hard on this order and would like to get it to your expectations. If you can briefly explain what you want changed or fixed, we can work to rectify the situation." I can't tell you how many times I have used this response while going on a long walk to cool off. It's a great way to buffer time and keep everything professional.

- **Step away from the computer.** Half the time, I would fire out angry responses back to clients and hours later wish I hadn't. If I had paused for a few hours before responding, all the trouble would have been avoided. Naturally, angry clients don't want to wait hours to hear from you—they want a response immediately. That's why you're going to click on the presaved response and step away from the computer. Go for a walk, calm your mind, and cool off. You can even open a blank Word doc, vent in writing, and then delete it if you want. Do *not* draft this venting message in the original email chain, just in case you hit that "Send" button. Give yourself some time before you sit down to go through their actual revision.

- **Get Fiverr or the freelancing platform involved.** If a client is making your brain melt, you don't have to endure it alone. It took me awhile to realize this. Message Fiverr's customer service (or any platform's) and alert them to the angry client who wants to cancel the order. They will get back to you and help mediate the situation. Alerting them ahead of time shows them you care about the order and keeping the client happy. If the client still pushes 200% to cancel the order, Fiverr may compensate you regardless. Give Fiverr (or the platform you're using) a chance to be on your side by communicating with them early on.

As a human, you also need a place to vent. Facebook groups and other online communities are great outlets where you can post about unfortunate freelancing situations. Be sure you are in closed or private groups so you can vent in privacy.

Overall, don't resent or make fun of your clients. They are just as much a part of your business as you are. Learn to work in harmony with them. It'll be a much easier process if you can set your pride aside.

In Chapter 7, we're going to look at the upper echelons of freelancing platforms, and why titles like Fiverr PRO can launch you into the six-figure realm. More than anything, customer service is especially important if you want to rake in thousands per day on freelancing sites.

Chapter 6 Key Points

- Customers are a necessary part of your business, so learn to live in peace with them.
- The happier you make a customer, the more they are going to buy from you.
- Presaved responses will be your best friend in customer disputes.
- Anticipate occasional angry clients so you aren't caught off-guard.

7 The Upper Echelons of Freelancing Platforms

If you're not willing to risk the unusual, you will have to settle for the ordinary.

— Jim Rohn

In 2017, something life changing happened to me. Fiverr called me in to film a commercial in Greenpoint, Brooklyn. At this point in my life, this was probably the coolest thing that had ever happened to me. A major international company wanted me to be in their commercial—wow. I agreed to it instantly and showed up a few weeks later on a gloomy, drizzly day. The shoot was set to happen inside one of the warehouses north of Williamsburg. That was basically all Fiverr had told me at the time.

As I went inside, I saw a few other Fiverr sellers and a big crew set up with a stool in the middle of a dark gray industrial room. I stood around for a bit and finally mustered up the courage to ask one of the Fiverr staffers what the commercial was going to focus on. He looked at me and went, "Oh! They haven't told you yet? You are filming for the launch of Fiverr PRO."

I stared at him, puzzled, and blurted out, "Um, what is Fiverr PRO?"

He laughed, knowing this program was going to change my life long before I did. He responded, "It's going to be the top 1% of the platform. It's the premier program that's going to put Fiverr on the map for having the best freelancing talent in the world."

I paused for a minute with my thoughts racing. My brain was trying to do the math. If I was going to be in a program for the top 1% of the platform, did that mean I was going to make more money? My eyes were wide. When they finally called me up to sit on the stool, I asked the director, "Does this mean I am going to be charging more for my services?" He laughed and said, "Oh, honey, yes. They are going to benchmark your rates for at least $100, minimum."

At the time, I was charging $15 to $25 for my basic packages. It was working out well for me—I closed out 2017 having made $67,000. Not bad for a freelance writer at a random Starbucks.

Hearing the $100 figure made me almost faint. I wanted to run around the block, call my mom, and scream with joy. But I had to remain focused and film this damn commercial. My subconscious brain started to whisper to me, "You're going to be making four times what you made this year in 2018."

That . . . that would mean I was going to make over $200,000 freelance writing, from my laptop, at home. No way, not possible, I told myself.

Fast forward to 2018 when Fiverr PRO finally came out of beta, and that six-figure dream became a reality, quickly. By

June 2018, I had made $150,000 in six months, spurring the first CNBC story that changed my life yet again (for better and for worse). Since then, the program has made me a consistent $250,000 to $400,000 every single year. In some ways, it still feels like a dream.

Except it's not. It's a very real program that you can apply to and become part of. I have seen it happen hundreds of times over with my students and Facebook group members. Fiverr PRO is not an elusive, exclusive club that only a few dozen people get to access. They accept people into the program weekly—trust me. Therefore, Fiverr PRO should become one of your top goals as a new freelancer. And better yet, you don't have to wait three years to join it—I have seen countless freelancers get accepted after just a few months using the platform.

What Is Fiverr PRO?

Fiverr PRO is a separate platform from the regular Fiverr marketplace, and it offers clients the best talent Fiverr has to offer. Although Fiverr has its ranking system (New Level, Level 1, Level 2, and Top Level), Fiverr PRO is a separate designation. It's considered to be the top 1% of the platform, which is why clients are more than happy to pay expensive rates. In fact, Fiverr demands that you charge expensive rates to contribute to the idea that the clients are buying "designer" services with Fiverr.

Fiverr PRO contains fewer selling categories than regular Fiverr, although they do add categories monthly to the program. In order to open new Fiverr PRO gigs, Fiverr must approve your "expertise" in the category. They do this by having you fill out an extensive application when you apply to be part of the program. If they deny your application, you can reapply unlimited times. There is really no risk in seeking out Fiverr PRO participation.

Current Fiverr PRO categories include Graphics & Design, Digital Marketing, Writing & Translation, Video & Animation, Music & Audio, Programming & Tech, and Business.

Fiverr still collects their flat 20% fee for all Fiverr PRO transactions. That can hurt at times, especially when it's a $1,000+ order. In those moments when I feel frustrated, I do remember that Fiverr is supplying me with a steady stream of clients I do not have to go out and find myself. As mentioned in previous chapters, there are pros and cons to being dependent on a company marketplace. But in the case of Fiverr PRO, the pros (earnings) outweigh the cons (20% fees and ceding to Fiverr's rules). Or at least that's how I feel.

Doing the Math

In general, Fiverr PRO sellers earn around $200/hour for their work on Fiverr. That means working only a few hours per day to earn what is a very comfortable living in the Western world. I know plenty of Fiverr PRO sellers who work just two hours per day, traveling the rest of the day in countries with lower standards of living. This enables them to live like kings and queens, while working a 10- to 12-hour workweek. Not bad at all.

I would be remiss if I did not point out the pressure that comes with making this kind of money, of course. The clients are generally higher quality if they have big budgets; yet, they expect you to work for that money. They are not going to tolerate typos or innocent mistakes. And they are certainly not going to tolerate late deliveries. They expect the utmost professionalism from you, in both your delivery and customer service. In a way, can you blame them?

Therefore, I recommend everyone get at least a few months of experience on a site like Fiverr before you apply to PRO. It's not going anywhere. You want to have some basis of customer service acumen and time management before you get thrown into the Fiverr PRO marketplace.

Upwork, Other Platforms, and the Myth of Saturation

If Fiverr has a Fiverr PRO, then Upwork of course has an equivalent. Upwork distinguishes its top 1% of freelancers through a badge labeled "Expert-Vetted." Expert-Vetted freelancers must go through a thorough pre-screening by "experts in their field," according to Upwork. The freelancers are also evaluated by the Upwork Technical Talent Managers for their expertise and soft skills. At this time, freelancers in Web, Mobile, and Software Development; Design and Creative; and Sales and Marketing can become Expert-Vetted.

Any Fiverr or Upwork competitor in the future will follow suit with their premiere 1% program if they want to be competitive. The freelancing marketplace competition only favors us, the freelancers. As they battle it out for market share, we get to capitalize from their specialized programs that compensate us handsomely. And remember: if you're rejected from these programs at first, don't lose hope. Apply again, and again, and again. There's no harm in going after what you want with urgency!

Don't let the fancy names and titles of these programs intimidate you. These marketplaces need a fresh new flow of expertise to keep their clients happy. Freelancers may shut down their profiles, move in another direction, open an agency and drift off the marketplaces, or slowly phase out of it. Don't get caught up in the idea of "saturation" and thinking there is no room for you. Millions of businesses are going online every single day, and they need dozens of freelancers to help them make the digital pivot. As Jon Younger wrote in *Forbes* (Younger 2021) in 2021: "The Freelance Revolution Has a Supply Problem, Not a Demand Problem."

Saturation doesn't exist for freelancers who commit themselves to being the very best they can be at their craft. Get out there, start freelancing, open freelancing profiles, and launch an agency. Fall in love with your work, and don't concern yourself with what other freelancers are doing. It's always wise to keep an eye on the competition, but their freelancing business isn't detracting from yours. Run your own race, and you'll find the world of freelance buying is as alive as ever.

As you start to secure a steady flow of freelancing income, you're going to have surplus money. What should you do with that money? How can you use this monetary momentum to achieve the end goal: financial freedom? It starts with side hustles. Next, we are going to look at the explosion of side hustles, options available to you, and how you can set up passive income streams that churn along in your sleep. We're going to look at how you can build out an entire virtual team that steers the side-hustling ship while you venture off to the Caribbean for three weeks with no cell service.

See you in Part II. And remember what T. S. Eliot said: "Only those who will risk going too far can possibly find out how far one can go."

Chapter 7 Key Points

- Every freelancer should strive to join a top 1% program on a freelancing platform.

- Fiverr PRO is how I went from making $67,000 per year to $250,000+.

- It's easier to get into these programs than you might think. Keep trying!

- Freelancing saturation is a myth.

II Side Hustling

8 Breaking Down Your Freelancing Income

Only those who will risk going too far can possibly find out how far one can go.

— T. S. Eliot

It's common to plan only one to two weeks in advance when getting started with something as brand-new as freelancing. We get caught up in the short term, dedicating every ounce of our focus to making sure this newfound side hustle is successful. I was the exact same way for a very long time.

Looking back, if I could change one thing about my freelancing journey, it would be to scale my business, prices, and goals more quickly. I was beyond happy making a few thousand dollars per month for years. And it is not lost on me that billions of people around the world would give anything to have that be a reality for themselves. I am eternally grateful every day.

But, as the Law of Attraction, principle of manifestation, and plain ol' prayer goes, you will only achieve what you believe is possible for yourself. You must dream bigger, press on, and truly see yourself as someone who is deserving of more. There is nothing wrong with wanting more—no one else is going to "want more" for you. Only you can make that a reality for yourself—I can't stress it enough!

As the months wear on while you grow your freelancing business, something amazing is going to happen: you're going to have some leftover money. At first, it may just be $50 here and there. But if you believe it's possible, soon it can become an extra $5,000 or $10,000. I have had countless guests on my podcast go over how they made over $100,000 their very first year freelancing.

Now, that doesn't have to be your goal at all. The beauty of this is that you can freelance part-time if you want. The gig economy is a place where you don't have to work yourself to death; it's the antithesis of the 40-hour corporate work week. People are burnt out and want a different reality for themselves.

But, even when you're working as a freelancer part-time, it's not uncommon to earn around $5,000/month working 15- to 20-hour weeks. Based on the average cost of living for an American (we will be using this as the example throughout this chapter), $5,000 will leave you with plenty of leftover money that you can now leverage to ensure your remote working legacy. Let's look at the math.

What Is a Real Freelancing Profit?

Every day I sign onto my social media and see a comment from someone, anywhere in the world, saying, "Yeah, but you're posting your money stats before considering your costs. You're only posting revenue."

It makes me want to teleport to where they are to have some tea with them and explain why freelancing is so amazing: there are barely any costs associated with it. What little business schooling we did receive growing up went over the big business terms everyone throws around in conversation today: profit, loss, revenue, cash flow, taxes, debits, and credits. I see those words used hourly in comments that critique my social media content. Don't get me wrong, those words are all important when used in the right context. However, getting caught up in business jargon isn't necessary in the Wild West of making money online today. All you need to be concerned with is securing a computer of some kind (don't forget that public libraries do provide computer access for free), WiFi (free WiFi can be found in many fast food and coffee chains), and time (thankfully, time is a free commodity equally distributed to every person on planet earth).

If you have those three things, you're in business. That means that your only real costs associated with freelancing online today are the one-time cost of buying a computer (can range from $500 to $2,000), the recurring cost of paying for WiFi (can range from $50 to $150/month), and let's say you want to also use a smartphone when managing your business (most plans are around $80–$100/month when paying off fancy phones). If we break down the cost of the laptop (we'll go with $1,500) over its lifetime of, let's say, five years (or 60 months), it comes to about $25/month. Add that to $100 for WiFi and $90 for your phone, and you come to about $215/month to run a highly effective freelancing business that does not rely on any other businesses, libraries, or Starbucks to make it a reality.

When you take your $5,000/month in freelancing revenue and subtract the $215, you are barely scratching the surface of your hard-earned money. Coming in at $4,785, that's still a very handsome salary that is going to create a comfortable and agile life for you and your family.

Better yet, no matter how much you increase your freelancing prices, these costs stay constant. If you're making $15,000/month, your costs are still $215 per month. Name another business in which the costs are not only this low, but also remain constant no matter how much you scale your business! I'll wait.

My point here is that the costs of freelancing are minuscule compared to its potential. In the past, it was impossible for a business to operate like this. It's only possible thanks to the limitlessness of the internet, and the ability for you to be in multiple places at one time through technology.

Now, stick with me here, I know the math is getting dense (I don't like numbers either). Let's compare this average freelancing salary with the average cost of living in a U.S. city today.

Calculating Leftover Freelancing Income

We're going to use Tampa Bay, Florida, as the example here. As a Floridian myself, I feel Tampa is a great example—it's a massively expanding metropolis with tons of new construction, businesses, and moderately priced homes. Based on research presented by TampaBay.com (Martin 2016), the average Tampa resident pays around $978/month in principal, interest, taxes, and insurance on a median-priced home. Let's say that groceries cost $100/week, coming to $400 for the month. Let's say the person spends another $200/month going out to eat/entertainment. And suppose the person needs around

$350/month for utilities like electric, lawn services, internet, and phone payments.

Totaling around $1,928 at this point, let's figure that there are another $200 or so of unplanned expenses or events that happen in the month. And let's also figure that there is a car payment of $300/month, plus gas costs of around $200/month, as well as health insurance premiums totaling around $200/month (we will go over health insurance for freelancers and how the cost is proportionate to income when using healthcare.gov later in this book). That comes to a grand total of $2,828. If the freelancer is taking home $5,000/month (this is pre-cost since WiFi and phone plans were factored into the utilities expenses earlier), they are left with a little over $2,000 to do whatever they want with it.

When I hit a point where I was starting to save a couple of thousand dollars per month, I wasn't sure exactly what to do with it. I knew I should be saving for retirement, but I also knew interest rates in savings accounts were dismal. I knew there were better ways I could be growing my money, yet I was only 24 years old. Society told me I was "too young to know how to responsibly manage my own money." So, I did what probably anyone else in my shoes would have done: I sat on it and did nothing. I did this for a few years. Now, retrospectively, I understand how inflation works today. I understand that doing nothing with your money means you're losing money. But I didn't know what the hell I wanted to do with the money when it was coming in.

I don't want you to feel like a deer in headlights just because I did. That's why we're preparing for you to have this surplus cash now. If you can envision it, it will surely become your reality. What exactly should you do with an extra $2,000 lying around every month?

Taxes tip: your CPA will advise you to set aside 30 to 40% of your freelancing income for estimated tax payments. Every three months, I send a payment to the IRS based on what my total tax burden was for the year prior. I divide the total by four and send that amount quarterly to the IRS before it's tax time. This ensures you are not caught in a situation where you owe more in taxes than you presently have saved. Saving up to 40% of what you earn for taxes will put you in a very safe and comfortable position. But, again, I am not a professional tax advisor, so I recommend seeking out the support of a CPA if you plan to make this your reality.

Reinvesting into Your Expanding Empire

For legal purposes, I am not a financial advisor. I am not providing financial advice, nor am I telling you exactly how to use your money. But I am going to share what I did with my money, and how it has been able to triple and quadruple itself for me by putting it into more active markets as opposed to decaying savings accounts.

Today, my money is split out into an IRA, a Self-Employment Pension Fund, cryptocurrency (mainly Ethereum), two investment properties in the state of Florida, and the rest back into my other side hustles. We are going to look at a more detailed breakdown of how my money is allocated in forthcoming chapters, but for the purpose of this one, I want to talk about taking your money and investing it into additional side hustles. Why settle for one burgeoning online business when you can have 10? This is a common theme in my social media content. We've been so conditioned to think it's normal to have just one income for the entirety of your life until you can retire, sit around, and die. We trade off 40 years of our life relying on one singular source of income. I say to that, "No thank you!" Why weren't we taught that with technology, virtual assistants, and software, we can have six, eight, even 12 sources of income? Talk about the ultimate form of financial security!

With the extra few thousands of dollars you have every month, you can start setting up additional streams of income for yourself. In this part of the book, we are going to look at additional side hustle options, vetting virtual assistants, managing your time, and identifying the right hustles for you. Many of these side hustles can be launched with just a few extra hundred dollars you have at your disposal now. Costs associated with running your own business off of freelancing platforms can be buying a domain ($50 to $1,000, depending on the name), building a website, or paying someone to do it for you ($1,000 to $5,000, depending on the expansiveness of the website), paying a copywriter to write the content for you ($50/500 words is standard), hosting packages on sites like WordPress ($120/year typically), working with a CPA to prepare your taxes ($600/year and one of the best investments you could ever make in yourself), and running ads to whatever it is you are selling ($25 to $10,000/month, depending on how big your business is).

These kinds of side hustles, like affiliate marketing or drop shipping, come with a few more startup costs when compared to freelancing on marketplaces. That's why I recommend you consider these side hustles after you've established a consistent business with freelancing. I also recommend that you take it slowly: don't try to open 10 side hustles in two months.

Establish your freelancing business for a few months, gain confidence, and then start to invest in one additional side hustle. Get that one off the ground, wait a few months again, and repeat the process. This was my formula and so far, it has worked out amazingly.

In Chapter 9, I go over the top 10 side hustles to consider for yourself in the present day, their pros and cons, and how to pick the side hustles that are right for you, your interests, your skill set, and your available time. There is a reason the average millionaire has at least seven different streams of income (Minton n.d.)!

Chapter 8 Key Points

- Freelancing comes with minuscule costs when compared to any other business today.
- Working only part-time hours can still produce $5,000/month in freelancing revenue.
- Freelancing can quickly create surplus income that you can use to reinvest into other side hustles.
- Start slow, establish your freelancing business, and then move onto launching one side hustle at a time.

9 Top Ten Side Hustles to Consider

Never depend on a single income. Make investments to create a second source.

— Warren Buffett

Thanks to technology and the interconnectedness of living in a 5G world, you can have as many side hustles today as you can conceivably want. There are more side hustle options available to you than you can possibly imagine, which is what makes living right now so interesting—it's never been easier for people around the world to access money online. It's making distribution of money more equitable in a lot of ways, if you take the initiative, of course, to work hard and go find it.

I've tried my hand at a lot of different side hustles at this point. I am fascinated by the odds-and-ends jobs across the internet that can accrue hundreds of dollars every month. I would go as far to say it's one of my hobbies to read up on side hustles and attempt them myself. Since I am merely a mortal, I have had just as much failure with my side hustles as I have had success. The failures were simply because I discovered it wasn't a side hustle I enjoyed doing or automating. But there is only one way for you to discover the same—you must get your hands dirty and test it out yourself.

With a successful and reliable freelancing business humming in the background, you will have the confidence to try your hand at these side hustles and entertain the idea that they might fail. You'll have that luxury knowing your other business is making a few thousand dollars per month. I am never advocating for anyone to make insanely risky financial decisions.

The list in this chapter is a collection of side hustles I can personally vouch for as being lucrative and manageable, as well as side hustles that acquaintances and friends of mine have had notable success with. In Chapter 10, we will go over how to pick the right side hustle for yourself.

Work as an Online Tutor

The world of online education is exploding. E-learning is expected to reach a valuation of $350 billion (Tannenbaum n.d.) by 2025. Thanks in part to the COVID-19 pandemic, schools, students, and companies discovered that education can be proctored over the internet effectively. Even better, studies proved that employees were more productive (in 2022) and happier working from home, doing the same jobs they were managing in an office setting.

Therefore, one of the simplest side hustles that you can manage from home (or on the road) is online tutoring. Tutors can earn up to $75/hour on sites like Fiverr and Upwork providing their services in a variety of topics, from arithmetic and linguistics, to coding and marketing. The traditional topics taught in school only account for a fraction of the online tutoring market today. Tutoring focused specifically on different testing prep is in high demand.

- **Sites to use:** TutorMe, Tutor.com, Wyzant, Fiverr, Upwork, LinkedIn, and Preply
- **Materials needed:** Laptop, WiFi
- **Skills needed:** Ability to teach knowledge and work with students of different backgrounds

Sell Online Courses

On the same topic of e-learning as tutoring is the massively expanding industry of online courses. I can't tell you how many online courses I have not only developed for my own sales, but have also taken this year. Online courses are the gateways to learning about YouTube, SEO, mining crypto, selling NFTs, becoming an influencer, affiliate marketing, and so many other lucrative online endeavors today. On good days, my online course packages can make upwards of $2,000. Even if you sell one online course for $300/sale, that one sale can totally change your monetary life. I choose to keep my price packages low, since my courses are based on a subscription model.

Unlike freelancing and tutoring, online course sales can be passive. Every so often, I use active engagement to make the courses themselves (with my course business partner). But once they are done, uploaded, and available for purchase, you can sell them in your sleep. Passive income should be one of your main remote economy goals as you go through this journey.

- **Sites to use:** Udemy, Skillshare, Teachable, Podia, and Thinkific. Note: my courses are sold from my own website, which I own. I do this because I drive a lot of my traffic from my social media accounts. If you don't plan to post to social media, use one of the sites listed here.

- **Materials needed:** Laptop, a camera (nicer cameras are around $2,000), some professional lighting (I use two Lumix lights that were around $175/each), and professional audio recording equipment (you can use a Bluetooth Yeti mic or wireless audio tools that total around $300). Note: these are essential tools for recording anything, whether it be social media content, YouTubes, or podcasts. Investing in these tools can help you launch additional side hustles. It's worth it to splurge for the best in media production.

- **Skills needed:** Demonstrated experience in any field, ability to talk clearly to camera, video editing

Sell ebooks

Back in 2018 when the first CNBC piece came out on my story, I had zero products to my name. I panicked as thousands of people poured onto my social media and I had nothing to sell. What kind of entrepreneur was I? I locked myself in my room (not actually) for about one week and wrote an ebook on Fiverr basics. I made a cover in Canva, hired someone on Fiverr to edit it, and uploaded the ebook to Amazon Kindle Publishing one week later. I also opened my own website (alexfasulo.com) and listed the ebook there as well for a cheeky price of $5 (a play on the name Fiverr).

Today, I make around $30/day doing absolutely nothing. I haven't touched that ebook since 2018. I sell a couple of copies every single day to people around the world, making ebooks one of my favorite sources of passive income. And there is no rule saying you must stop with just one ebook. You could publish an entire library of 20 ebooks, priced around $5. If you sold every single one of them just once per day . . . that's $100/day from doing nothing once they are published.

- **Sites to use:** Word Doc or Google Docs to write the ebook (or hire a copywriter on Fiverr or Upwork to write it for you), Amazon KDP for uploading the ebook for sale, Canva for designing the cover for free.
- **Materials needed:** Laptop, WiFi.
- **Skills needed:** Ability to write and edit decently (otherwise, outsource to a copywriter), graphic design to create a fun cover (you can outsource this as well), and patience uploading the ebook to Amazon.

Start a Blog

If you think the blogging market is saturated, think again. Content continues to grow in importance for marketing purposes today, since most of us are doing our shopping online. If you are passionate about a certain subject, a blog can be a great way to profit off ads, sponsorships, and affiliate marketing links.

Better yet, you don't need to be a Shakespeare with your words. You can hire freelancers to edit your content, or even outsource the blog writing entirely to these copywriters (as a freelancer, this is in essence how I made all that Fiverr money)! Consistency is important if you want to be successful with this, so aiming to publish at least one piece of new content every week is required. Collaborate and link to other bloggers to get more visitors on your page. Open a Facebook page or group centered around your blog and build an audience that visits your blog weekly.

From just website clicks and views alone, your blog can make $1,000/month+ in just a few months. You can automate the entire thing by outsourcing the writing, and even a hire a virtual assistant who uploads the new blogs and updates the website for you.

- **Sites to use:** WordPress is regarded as the best for this, but other sites like Wix and Squarespace are available
- **Materials needed:** Laptop, WiFi
- **Skills needed:** Basic writing, editing, and graphics and design (you can outsource it all if you don't have these skills)

Launch a YouTube Channel

Remember all that media production equipment listed earlier? If you went ahead and bought it, you can become a YouTube star. Even if you haven't purchased it, you can still get started on YouTube. Technically, you only need a smartphone, some WiFi, and an idea. This is how I started out my channel—nothing but me, some horrible lighting, my phone, and topics on Fiverr. Funnily enough, some of my first YouTube videos with terrible production quality make me $10–$20 every day in AdSense revenue. Value > everything else. Remember that!

You will need 1,000 subscribers and 4,000 hours of channel watch time before you can monetize your channel. Once you reach this benchmark, you can enable ads on your videos. Google will pay you for those views. At 28,000 subscribers, my channel makes around $600/month from views. And that's not including brand partnerships and sponsorship links in the captions of the videos. Brands can give you affiliate links and pay you a commission every time someone clicks a link in your YouTube description. In this way, one YouTube video can make you money for years without your ever having to touch it again. After Google, YouTube is the second most powerful search engine on the internet. There is undoubtedly room for you.

- **Sites to use:** iMovie, Splice, or any other video editing software, YouTube
- **Materials needed:** Camera, lights, audio equipment, laptop, smartphone, and somewhere with a nice video backdrop setting
- **Skills needed:** Talking to camera, video editing (I outsource this to a video editor), graphics (I outsource my YouTube thumbnails), YouTube SEO (tons of free videos on YouTube explain this)

Start Affiliate Marketing

What was once scoffed at for being a "scammy" way to make money online has become one of the most lucrative digital industries in existence today. Brands know that affiliate marketing can make their products much more appealing when compared to outdated advertising campaigns. They issue links to their products that you use to promote whatever it is they are selling. Each company has a different commission program—some of them will even send you gifts and plaques for reaching certain thresholds.

Adrian Brambila, who is a good friend of mine, famously reached a $4 million net worth (Maidan 2021) through nothing but affiliate marketing. He works as an affiliate for dozens of brands by using blogs, advertisements, and social media content to see their products. Affiliate marketing perfectly complements a YouTube channel or starting your own blog—you use these links inside your other side hustles to make you more money. It's side hustling inception at its finest!

- **Sites to use:** Your own websites, Wix/WordPress, YouTube, TikTok, ShareASale Affiliates, Amazon Affiliates, eBay Partners, Clickbank, Shopify Affiliate Program
- **Materials needed:** Laptop, WiFi
- **Skills needed:** Ability to run paid ads (or outsource it), blog writing (which can be outsourced), time management

Become an Influencer

The word "influencer" doesn't mean what it used to mean today. It's not just a woman, ages 18 to 28, trying on different clothes and posting on travel trips. An influencer is someone who commands a following of at least a few thousand people, and it can be based on virtually anything. I know influencers who have followings because they go live and eat food on camera. Others, like myself, have followings because we educate people every day on certain topics. You can build a following around literally anything. There is even a guy I follow on TikTok who drinks water out of a hamster water bottle. It's intriguingly bizarre, and I can't look away.

Beyond the creativity, influencing pays well. Really well. Influencers with 30,000–60,000 followers on TikTok charge $1,500 per video, and $3,000 per Reel with similar followings on Instagram. You can have as few as 5,000 followers on these apps and still charge $200–$500 per video you post for brands. Having the following I do on social media apps, I can charge $6,000+ per post I do for brands. Not to say it isn't hard work—there is a lot of back and forth/revising that goes on. But still, the pay is incomparable, and the traffic you will be able to drive from your social media to your other side hustles is invaluable.

My ebook sales, course sales, and soon-to-be book sales will come predominantly from my social media following.

To get started, pick two social media apps (I recommend Pinterest and TikTok) and start posting multiple pieces of content per day. Don't worry about editing it to perfection. People want authenticity. Be yourself, teach something, read a book, or eat a meal. Film it, post it, and interact with your followers every single day. Ask them what they want to see from you—post polls on your Instagram Stories. I am doing this as I write this book. People love to feel included and heard.

- **Sites to use:** TikTok, Pinterest, YouTube, Instagram, Facebook, Twitch, Twitter
- **Materials needed:** Smartphone, WiFi
- **Skills needed:** Authenticity on camera, dismantling of one's pride, consistency, some video editing in apps like Splice

Become an Airbnb Host

Airbnb can sound daunting. I get it. You're probably thinking you need to go buy some property with 3.5% down and hope that it rents. Although that's certainly an option, there are less risky ways to get into Airbnb. For starters, there is Airbnb arbitrage, which is when you take out a lease with a landlord that allows you to rent the property on Airbnb. This is most successful with a corporate lease, FYI. Additionally, do you have a spare room in your home that you don't use? Is it possible to put a door somewhere in that room leading outside so your guests have a private entrance? You can Airbnb rooms in your home, bungalows, or creative yurts, treehouses, and even teepees on your property. Be sure to check with local zoning laws and regulations to make sure you aren't violating any rules.

Once you have your listing finalized, take professional photos (if you don't trust yourself with this, it is worth it to hire a local photographer) and make your Airbnb listing. You can use software like Airdna (www.airdna.co/) to look up the median Airbnb price in your area, as well as a slew of other details to help make your listing competitive. Decorate the space with fun furniture that lends itself to great Instagram posts. Activate your listing and plan to either take care of cleaning the sheets yourself or working with a local cleaning company that does it for you.

I know plenty of people who are making $20,000+ per month with Airbnb, working only 5–10 hours per week managing the listings. These people, of course, have multiple listings and own some of the properties. But we all must start somewhere.

- **Sites to use:** Airbnb, Vrbo, Airdna, social media to promote the listings
- **Materials needed:** A physical space to rent, fun furniture/décor, camera
- **Skills needed:** Good customer service when messaging guests, eye for design, attentiveness to Airbnb app

Launch a Podcast

I'll be honest, I did not want to launch my own podcast in 2021. I personally did not listen to any podcasts at the time, and I thought it was going to be just another content demand on my day. Boy, was I wrong. Podcasting has been transformative for my business and has created more revenue streams than I could have imagined. Not only do brands pay for ads at the beginning, middle, and end of your podcast, but they will also pay to have you link to them in the captions. Even better, I can have my business idols on the podcast and get to know them. I am launching a few businesses this year with some of my podcast guests. I would say the networking ability that comes from podcasting is unlike anything else you could be doing today.

With a podcast that has only around 20,000–40,000 downloads (this is very doable if you consistently record and post every week for a few months), brands will spend $300–$600 for different ad packages. I am still in the beginning stages with my podcast, but it has gotten me media coverage, brand deals, and business partnerships I would have never had without it.

I was intimidated when first starting out. I realized you only need a nice Bluetooth Yeti mic that you plug into your laptop. Record the podcast for free in Audacity (www.audacityteam.org/). I use an audio editor for $50/episode who cleans it up for me. But you can always do it yourself. I then post the episodes to RSS.com (free). It syndicates to Spotify, Apple Podcasts, and other major streaming sites for me! Tons of people started following me on Instagram from my podcast today.

- **Sites to use:** Riverside.fm, Spotify Podcasts, RSS.com, Audacity, Zoom
- **Materials needed:** Laptop, WiFi, one microphone
- **Skills needed:** Ability to write podcast scripts and/or speak naturally into a microphone, authentic personality

Start a Dropshipping Business

Finally, we have dropshipping. Ecommerce is exploding with money today, and successful dropshippers are earning $60,000/month (many times more), especially around the holidays. I saved this side hustle for last because I want to be honest about the risk that comes with it. I tried out two dropshipping brands myself. You must front a lot of money to buy your stock that will be shipped to your future buyers. There is risk in buying an inventory without knowing if it will be purchased. You also must pay for the ads that run the business. Facebook changed up its ads policy last year and it took down a lot of dropshippers.

Still, the process of selling products to online shoppers without having to ever process the product itself is revolutionary. That's what dropshipping is. Your supplier will ship out the product for you, as you, when an order is placed on your website. It's up to you to set up the website, buy the domain, come up with a catchy name and logo, populate the website, and start selling. Your buyers will be driven to the site via ads. If you are not comfortable running ads, you may want to outsource this part of the business. But with bigger risk comes bigger reward. Though dropshipping has monetary risk, it can make you a ton of business. My first dropshipping brand was selling VR headsets. I was making around $3,000–$5,000 per month after the costs were factored in. I found it required too much of my time after a while. That doesn't mean it can't work for you, though.

- **Sites to use:** AliExpress, AliBaba, SaleHoo, Megagoods, Wholesale Central, SquareSpace, WordPress
- **Materials needed:** Laptop, smartphone, WiFi, WhatsApp (how most suppliers prefer to communicate), lots of startup money

Which side hustle is right for you? What amount of risk do you want to stomach? I can't necessarily answer these questions for you, but I can walk you through the process of identifying the right side hustles to integrate into your growing empire. Let's check it out in Chapter 10.

Chapter 9 Key Points

- There is an infinite number of side hustles to try out today.
- The only way to know which side hustles are right for you is to get your hands dirty and dive in.
- Prioritize starting side hustles that can become passive income.
- Bigger risk comes with bigger reward in the world of side hustling.

10 Picking the Right Side Hustles for You

Good things happen to those who hustle.

— Anaïs Nin

One of the most empowering—and detrimental—aspects of a freely accessible internet today is the paradox of too many choices. You can sift through thousands upon thousands of side hustles available at your disposal. There are hundreds of freelancing sites, millions of Facebook groups, and billions of websites. Even on a site like Fiverr.com, there are over 550 different services that can be offered by freelancers.

Sounds amazing, right? In the lens of opportunity, it has never been better. Yet too many choices can create a psychological phenomenon in which we either delay making a choice altogether, or we feel dissatisfied with the one we did make (Krockow 2018). It's why looking at a menu with over 100 different entrée options can, in a lot of ways, stress you out. We feel comfortable looking at a one-page menu, especially if we are sitting across the table from someone we are trying to engage with. It can feel overwhelming—I get it.

Understanding this psychological phenomenon when heading into the world of side hustling can help you avoid falling into one of the two traps listed earlier. Analysis paralysis prevents most people from engaging in the gig economy, overthinking the choices you could have made, or wondering if the one you did was the "right" one.

I want you to approach side hustling with an open mind. We're going to look at how to approach such a bustling and expansive industry so that you feel content, fulfilled, and confident in the decisions that you've made.

Breaking Down the Time You Have

When choosing what side hustle makes sense for you, the very first thing you should do is a time audit. Sit down and go over where you have pockets of free time in your days. Maybe you have a couple of hours hanging out in the morning, or a long lunch period. Maybe you get off from work at 5 p.m. and don't really have anything else to do before you fall asleep at 1 a.m. after bingeing Netflix. Maybe you have completely free weekends, or maybe you are a single parent trying to somehow make all this work with a child at home.

First, write down your estimate of the available time you have each day of the week. Once that's done, add it together for a grand total. Don't worry, even having just three free hours throughout the entire week can still lend itself to productive side hustling.

Now, I am going to push you out of your comfort zone. Ready? You are going to map out how you spend the rest of your time each day, down to 30-minute intervals. You may think you are busier than you actually are. I wouldn't be me if I didn't give you all a little tough love in this book. Write down how much time you spend sitting on social media, playing video games, watching Netflix, or, yes, even commuting (the remote work economy does not require commuting, saving participants dozens of hours every month).

This book is not designed to be part of that toxic hustle culture where writers encourage readers to hack their productivity and basically never have a social life again. I am merely asking you to become aware of how you spend your time. Let's say you estimate spending about 14 hours every week on social media and playing video games. My rule of thumb is trying to cut that 14 hours in half. That way, you're still leaving an hour every day for one of your time wasters, yet you have seven new hours you can now use on a side hustle. With seven hours used every week, you can manage just about any side hustle.

Add this new amount back to the amount you totaled at the top. I am going to guess your original total was around seven or eight hours, and it's now at the 15-hour mark. Good! The more time you can set aside for side hustling, the better.

Over time, once you master your side hustles and learn how to leverage software, chatbots, and virtual assistants to replace you, then you, too, can enjoy that four-hour workweek.

Analyzing Your Stomach for Risk

When compared to other forms of investment, side hustling in general is not particularly risky. Still, the risk required for different side hustles can vary greatly, which is why you want to think about how much of a risk-taker you really are.

When I was first starting out in the gig economy, I had zero stomach for risk. That's why I started with the least risky thing of all: freelancing. I did nothing but freelance for years. I didn't want to rock the boat. But, as I learned more and more about how money grows and wealth is accumulated, I realized some risk is required to really make that money work for you.

I started with less risky side hustles, like selling an ebook I wrote myself (saving the $500 cost associated with paying a freelancer to do it for you) and taught myself how to upload it to Amazon Kindle Publishing. Another year went by, and I finally decided to onboard my first freelance writer. Still, another year transpired, and I finally started to sell online course packages that I filmed with a videographer. It wasn't until 2020 that I really went for it with the "riskier" investments, like dropshipping/ecommerce and cryptocurrency.

Let's break down the 10 side hustles listed in Chapter 9 based on my perceived risk levels associated with them:

- **Risk Level: Easy**
  - ◆ **Online tutoring:** Freelancing is as risk averse as it comes.
  - ◆ **Starting a blog:** You can do this very cheaply if you make the blog yourself and buy a domain that's only $12–$50 for the year.
  - ◆ **Launching a podcast:** You can do this by signing up on a site like RSS.com for free and talking straight to your laptop or phone using a software like Audacity. If you want to hire audio editors and graphic designers to make your cover art, that can increase the "risk" associated with it.
  - ◆ **Become an influencer:** It has cost me $0 to become an influencer. It's hard work and requires consistency, but it costs nothing. All you need is a smartphone.

- **Risk Level: Moderate**

  - **Selling Online Courses:** Considerable production goes into selling online courses, so either plan to partner 50/50 with a videographer, or set aside some money to make this happen. You will then need to market the course to get sales.

  - **Selling ebooks:** If you outsource the writing/formatting of the book, ebooks can cost a moderate amount of money. You need to then market the ebooks to get sales.

  - **Launch a YouTube Channel:** You technically need a smartphone and a YouTube account to make this happen, costing you nothing. But, if you want to really leverage the account and make some serious sponsorship dollars, you will need a fair amount of electronics and some assistance with video editing.

  - **Become an Affiliate Marketer:** Running paid ads to your affiliate marketing campaigns can come with some risk if you are not familiar with managing ads online.

- **Risk Level: Hard**

  - **Starting a Dropshipping Business:** You will have to front the most amount of money when compared to other virtual side hustles. From time to time, you will also be communicating with suppliers that may have problems with communicating in English.

  - **Becoming an Airbnb Host:** Buying investment properties comes with a slew of risk. Yet, when done correctly, real estate + Airbnb can be a double investment that quickly sets you financially free.

These risk assignments are not permanent per side hustle. If you go with the DIY approach, many of them can be done for close to no money. It's up to you how "risky" you want to be with your initial investment dollars.

Identifying What Will Make You Happy

This isn't all about the money and financial freedom. Sure, those are some nice side effects, but this isn't corporate America. You can do what you want to do for a living. You can manage a side hustle that makes you feel fulfilled based on your personal interests, skill sets, and personality. You know the old saying: do what you love and never work a day in your life. That saying, from my experience, could not be truer.

How can you analyze your personality in a way that helps you pair up with the right side hustles? Instead of breaking this down in an introvert-vs.-extrovert way (I very much dislike how people use their self-identification as being introverted or extroverted as crutches when pursuing things today), let's look at some of the major personality traits needed to be successful in different kind of hustles:

- **Verbal/In-Person Customer Service:** Side hustles like being an Airbnb host and working with dropshipping suppliers is going to require you to be able to make a phone call and communicate with authority to the other person on the line. It may even require you to meet up with clients/partners in person.
- **Virtual Customer Service:** Freelancing is hugely based on virtual customer service. Being able to communicate with polite efficiency and proper email etiquette is important for freelancing and dropshipping/ecommerce clients.
- **Marketing/Social Media Marketing:** Being able to create marketing campaigns, content, and concepts is a very

creatively demanding endeavor: ebook sales, course sales, and influencing reach are largely based on marketing.

- **Sales:** Cold, hard sales pitches, landing pages, and outreach can be part of affiliate marketing, freelancing, and even blogging when reaching out to partner with other bloggers.

- **Editing/Refined/Detail-Oriented:** The finer, more intricate details are a massive part of managing a successful blog (no typos allowed), editing ebooks if you write them yourself, and video editing/script writing for YouTube.

- **Front-Facing Filming/Audio:** Podcasting, influencing, some forms of affiliate marketing, YouTubing, and filming online courses require you to get on camera. Fear not, if you have no prior experience doing this; remember, we all started at the same place.

Putting It All Together

Based on the personality attributes you consider yourself to have, you should be able to identify a few different side hustles that best align with your psyche. Remember: this is just my initial list of 10 proven side hustles based on my personal experience. There are so many other side hustles you can consider and bring through the process here when identifying if they are right for you.

After going through this three-step process, breaking down your time, analyzing your stomach for risk, and identifying your personality traits, a few side hustles above should be jumping out at you. Consider more than one side hustle when starting out—you may find yourself loving the side hustle you initially ruled out.

Regardless of the available time you have for your side hustles every week, time management is going to be incredibly important for maximizing every extra minute you have. Let's look at time management expectations so that you are not caught off guard when becoming an official side hustler.

Chapter 10 Key Points

- Every person is different when it comes to side hustles that are right for them.
- Start by calculating your available time every week.
- Analyze your stomach for risk and how much money you want to initially invest.
- Spend some time identifying your unique personality traits and how they align with the available side hustles.

11 Time Management Expectations

Time is the longest distance between two places.

— Tennessee Williams

This quote could not be more fitting for this chapter. You are going to have this idea in your head of what managing side hustles is going to look like—and then there is going to be the reality. The most amount of time these hustles demand from you is going to occur in those first few months. Over time, you may be able to cut down the time you once devoted to them by 80–90%. Like freelancing, if you really focus in the beginning on setting up side hustles that can hum along without you in the future, you are going to enter a state of financial freedom.

For the passive income side hustles like selling ebooks and online courses, the only time demand is going to happen in creating the product. Once it's done, perfected, uploaded, and available, you only need to worry about access to the product and directing traffic to that checkout button. In contrast, something like YouTubing can make you constant money from old video views; yet, if you want that money to stay the same or even grow, you are going to have to upload at least one video per week to the channel. The time demand remains constant, like podcasting.

Freelancing can be all consuming, or it can be entirely operational without you when you use an agency manager and virtual assistants. Virtual assistants can take over managing just about any side hustle for you, which is why we're going to look at how to vet virtual assistants and integrate them into your business in Chapters 13 and 14.

Virtual assistants, software, and automation can buy you back nearly 99% of your time if done correctly. And these tools will buy you back your time once you get your side hustles up and running with some level of success. I always believe you must get personal experience at the business for months and really know how it operates before you bring someone else in to do it for you.

Let's look at a general breakdown over your first year of side hustling when it comes to time management.

The Beginning: Months 1–4

There is no way to sugarcoat it: the first four months starting any side hustle are going to be the hardest. This period is going to demand the most amount of your time. You may need to devote two to three hours per day, even on weekends, to get your side hustle properly launched.

Do you have to devote this much time in the beginning? Not necessarily. The more time you put into the beginning of the business, the more quickly you are not only going to be turning a profit, but you will also be able to hire help that works in your absence. It's up to you how quickly you want to make this a lean, mean, money-making machine.

Note: if you followed the steps in Chapter 10 for picking the right side hustles for yourself, you should actually enjoy working on your side hustle. You should regard it as more of a hobby that feels fulfilling in some way. It should not feel like a stressful chore.

You can prepare for the first month to be the most frustrating. You are going to be watching a lot of YouTube videos and reading countless industry blogs on Google while you set up your system. This period of self-educating is going to be invaluable for you as a businessperson—it will increase your self-esteem and make you feel more empowered when starting new things. It will make all subsequent side hustle launches easier for you down the road.

After you feel you've acquired the necessary education, months 2, 3, and 4 will be able to insert it into the actual operation. You are going to have days of pure frustration. Something might not work the way you thought it would. You may want to give up a day or two. These are the critical days you must push through. It's how you crush the imposter syndrome right out of yourself. You may need to take a day or two off because your mind feels burnt out at times—that's okay. Listen to what your body needs!

When you make it to the very end of this initial period, congratulations, the worst is over! What are a few "intense" self-education months in the grand scheme of life? Nothing!

The Plateau: Months 5–8

By month 5, you can start scaling back the time your side hustles need every week. If you were previously dedicating 15 hours a week to making the hustle successful, you can consider scaling back to 10 hours per week. By this period, your side hustle should be generating some money, even if it's inconsistent or not what you had hoped for.

The plateau can be a boring side hustling period. Your business should, on some level, stay constant. It's the time to observe and work out the kinks and unexpected problems you could not have foreseen. You may have to make some decisions during this period to keep your business successful. Your newfound confidence from those first few months will be critical during this period. You may make some successful decisions, and some not-so-successful decisions. The failures are just as important—they are critical training opportunities. Learning more from these failures will set you up to onboard virtual assistants to the operation for the final period of automation.

This period should feel like a "plateau" in a lot of ways. Since it's still just you learning the business, you can't necessarily scale it yet. You should be exploring every inch of the side hustle so that you can train your incoming help with complete accuracy. You should also be working on refining your approach to marketing, social media, email marketing, or however you funnel your leads to your side hustle (see Chapters 9 and 10).

Spend this time watching even more YouTube videos, taking online courses, and reading books on the side hustles you have chosen. You never want to get complacent and think you know everything there is to know about a side hustle. Many of the industries in which these hustles operate change quickly. This change is what makes the virtual world of side hustling so accessible to new people—you don't want to wait 10 years to finally enjoy the fruits of your labor.

Just when you feel like you are starting to get bored, or are an expert on your side hustle, it's time to make things interesting.

The Automating: Months 9–12

It's the moment everyone has been waiting for: the automation. It's time to set up a real business that makes you money in your sleep. It's time to realize the four-hour work week everyone craves. It's a reward you can enjoy after months of working hard to perfect your side hustle.

In order to automate your side hustle, you are going to need two things: software systems and virtual assistants. Software, like copy.ai from example, can take a task you were previously doing, like freelance writing, and generate copy for you using an AI system (this has a long way to go; if you use AI in copywriting, you still need to go through the copy thoroughly, edit it, and add your human touch). Copy.ai can cut back your time by 50% yet still require editing that you can train virtual assistants to finish for you. Two amazing software tools you can use to make your knowledge infinitely accessible are Notion (the all-in-one planner/note-taking tool) and Loom (a screen-recording tool in which you can record your voice talking over a video).

With Notion and Loom, your virtual assistants can now understand how to run the portion of the business that software did not cover. We will go over this in more depth in Chapter 12.

It will take you from months 9 to 12 to really get your automation system into place. You will take a step back for a week and see how your team does without you. They will need a few weeks to really home in on any system weak spots, and they will need to be able to contact you frequently. Once you make it out of the trial-and-error period, you can, in essence, book a one-way flight to Bali and get ready to put only a few hours every week into your side hustle. Better yet, at this point your side hustle may be generating so much money that you consider it a main hustle. Fiverr started as a side hustle for me and quickly became my main career focus.

Be flexible in your side hustling outcomes. The time demands may not always be what you planned for. Adjust your expectations so you are not worried or surprised when you need to spend extra time. Identify a few ways to get back just three to four more hours per week that you don't feel you previously had. Maybe you can work out a carpool system in your neighborhood for getting your child to school. Maybe you can call your current job and ask to work 100% remotely at home to save on commuting. Sacrifices always must be made in some form to make any one of these money-making vessels work. I would be lying to you if I said it was all unicorns and rainbows! Think of the time sacrifice as an investment into your early financial retirement.

I know I just dangled a few carrots regarding automation tools and software products available to you today. In Chapter 12, I am going to break down the most productive, time-saving, and easy-to-use tools I use in my businesses every single day. These software products are truly the keys to financially free futures. I can't stress it enough!

Chapter 11 Key Points

- Be prepared to adjust your side hustling time management expectations slightly.
- The first few months setting up a side hustle are the hardest.
- If you stick with a side hustle to months 9 through 12, you can enjoy financial freedom.
- Don't be afraid to use tools, virtual assistants, and software to automate your side hustles after working to perfect them the first few months.

12 Automating Your Side Hustles for Passive Income

Contrary to popular opinion, the hustle is not a dance step—it's an old business procedure.

— Fran Lebowitz

It could be argued that the first form of automation happened in 1913 when Henry Ford invented the assembly line. Instead of a single craftsman assembling every element of a product or service, suddenly people were specializing in just one skill set they provided at a certain point in the car production process. It was a revolutionary unveiling that went on to change the world of manufacturing forever.

Before then, entrepreneurs either had to do everything themselves, or they needed to hire employees to help them with the business. Sure, this is one way to scale a business, and it is the model a lot of corporations use today. But the assembly line challenged how businesses operated. If machines mixed with specialized labor could suddenly crank out thousands of automobiles, why wouldn't every business want to operate on a similar level?

Fast-forward to today, and we have technology that Henry Ford would have given anything to access. We have computers, software, robots, chatbots, forms, and documents that can work for us, as us, on an infinite scale. As I write this book, someone can read through my different Notion documents I have embedded into my freelance marketplace on Facebook. My thoughts can exist infinitely, which makes it much easier to grow a business today than ever before in history.

To sum up Tim Ferriss's *The 4-Hour Workweek* (spoiler alert): we can work just a few hours per week and live all over the world because of automation. The man has leveraged every single automated tool, app, software, website, plug-in, and hybrid combination in how his businesses hum along in the background. He has made 20 different Tim Ferrisses who work at all hours of the day while he records podcasts with some of the most impressive people on the planet.

Tim was way ahead of his time, but this concept of automation integration into any side hustle is still central to financial freedom today. I would say even I have a long way to go in learning about all the different tools I could be embedding into my business. But I remain open and receptive to technology and have done my best to pass along any appealing software products to my agency manager and virtual assistants.

If there is one thing I want you to take away from this part of the book, it's the concept of automation. Reevaluate trading time for money, and instead, understand that technology can make you an infinite commodity. You don't necessarily even need to hire virtual assistants if you plan to automate 90% of your business. Automation should be at the center of how you plan to build out any kind of side hustle empire, no matter what it looks like. Also understand tasks that don't necessarily seem automatable, like personalized customer service, can still be largely automated. Automation is what gives today's internet entrepreneurs the advantage over individuals who stay at 9-to-5 jobs: they can only make as much as what time traded for money yields. They are not taking advantage of replicating themselves 100× over throughout their business funnels.

I don't blame people for not realizing how easy it really is to automate a side hustle today. This concept is still so new that when I explain it to people in person or on social media, they stare at me in confusion. It's very futuristic, the idea that you can take a certain thought or process of yours and make it immutable inside of a technological app. At the same time, it's incredibly exciting to think that the virtual version of you, or a thought process of yours, can live on long after you, changing the world on an infinite scale.

First, let's look at how I have approached automation in my business model, followed by the automation tools I recommend you use today.

How I Automate My Business

I started at square one, just like everyone else. It was just me, my MacBook, and a Fiverr account. I didn't have any special tools or the latest laptop at my disposal. I didn't have any money saved or really any idea of what I was doing. But I knew that an internet connection and time availability could get the job done—and that was all I needed to know.

I worked in this very bare-bones kind of model for years. If there is one thing I regret, it's how long it took me to realize that outsourcing/leveraging automation could transform my business. It's a scary thought, handing over the control of your business (your "baby" as many entrepreneurs call their businesses) to another person or entity. But before we talk, in Chapters 13 and 14, about the people at your disposal let's talk about handing over autonomy to technology.

The very first form of technology I integrated into my business came at the end of 2018 (yes, it took me three years to come around). I had an automated email system set up with my PayPal so when someone bought my ebook on my website, an email with the PDF of the ebook would be automatically sent to the person. Earning $50–$100/week from ebook sales without ever having to lift a finger had me hooked. I was finally making money without trading time.

In 2019, I started to experiment with MailChimp email marketing. MailChimp (https://mailchimp.com/) and other email software tools allow you to create form emails that are triggered at different parts in your funnel. For example, if someone signs up for my newsletter, my Flodesk (https://flodesk.com/) automatically sends them a welcome email that encourages them to check out some of my other resources, like my online courses. (I switched to Flodesk this year since it's more aesthetic in my opinion.) I have dozens of similar emails that keep people engaged in my brand, helping to build brand loyalty so they don't drift away.

That same year, I opened a Slack account (https://slack.com/). Slack is an excellent work communication chat tool where you can create different channels within your business. For example, I started my Slack with a channel for blogs, website content, ebooks, and editing. When I hired my first freelance writer, I would post the available jobs in their respective channels for him to mull over and decide if he wanted to take them or not. You could argue Slack isn't an "automation tool" in the way I used it, but it can be leveraged as one with recurring/pinned messages and its other slew of organization features.

I also had a chatbot developed for my Facebook account that responded back to any inquiry message. My Alexandra Fasulo public figure page would garner sizable attention every day, still due to the CNBC article that came out in 2018. The chatbot inside of my Facebook account was programmed to answer questions based on trigger words people sent. If they asked about my course, the chatbot would send them the link to my online course. Chatbots are now popularly used on websites, for customer service, inside of Instagram Direct Messages, and a slew of other places.

In 2020, that's when I really started to get serious with automation. I started to use Notion (www.notion.so/), the all-in-one notetaking, work assignment, organizer tool. I was able to dump everything I know about training freelancers into Notion, so that my future team could read it over and train themselves without me having to do the training every single time. I also started to use Loom (www.loom.com/), recording myself talking about the different tasks I would be onboarding people to do. Again, I wouldn't have to train people hands-on in the future, saving me a considerable amount of time.

This year, my team has been intensely leveraging Zapier (https://zapier.com/), which helps my agency manager to automate tedious sorting tasks as she assigns work to my freelancers. Zapier also helps my virtual assistants to keep emails organized and respond to inquiries more quickly. I have also purchased a Grammarly (www.grammarly.com/) business account that my writers can use to aid in their proofreading process. I find Grammarly to be accurate about 85% of the time. It does still require an extra proofreading on top of it if you plan to integrate it into your copywriting agency. Lastly, my team and I rely heavily on calendar-scheduling tool Calendly (https://calendly.com/), which enables my assistant to book out my schedule without checking in with me. I put in my available hours for the month ahead of time, and she can schedule my different appointments, lives, and podcasts based on available slots.

There are many more automation tools I want to carefully integrate into my business in the coming years. I truly believe that nearly 95% of my business model can be automated with the right tools. Therefore, I always recommend spending time testing out automation tools before you immediately sign up for them, buy them, and let them loose on your business. You want to tread with caution, since not all tools are created equal.

Automated Tools That You Should Consider

This is by no means a comprehensive list of every automated tool you should consider today. I could write an entire book on automation tools alone. Here are some of the biggest automation tools that entrepreneurs from every industry rave about on their social media and inside of their books:

- ActiveCampaign (www.activecampaign.com/): This all-in-one marketing tool combines advanced email marketing tools with a standard customer relationship management (CRM) tool. It integrates well with tools like Leadformly.

- Buffer (https://buffer.com/): I highly recommend checking out Buffer if you want to organize your social media content, posting schedule, and prioritize growing your social accounts.

- Constant Contact (www.constantcontact.com/): Another email marketing and automation tool, this software is easy to use for email newbies who want to grow their email list (growing your business email list should be one of your top priorities).

- Drip (www.drip.com/): One of the top marketing automation tools for eCommerce websites, Drip is a customer relationship management (CRM) software specifically for online stores.

- HubSpot (www.hubspot.com/): I have personally used this inbound marketing and sales software tool in the past. It makes it very easy to manage multiple social media channel campaigns, especially if you are running socials for multiple brands.

- IFTTT (https://ifttt.com/): Similar to Zapier, this automation tool makes it easy to create automations between different apps to save you the time opening dozens of tabs while repeating mundane tasks.

- Leadformly (https://leadformly.com/): Designed to increase form conversion rates, this tool helps you segment leads directly on web pages. The tool uses conditional logic to ask users questions based on what they type (a form of a chatbot), and then can send that information over to tools like ActiveCampaign.

- OptinMonster (https://optinmonster.com/): Touted as lead-generation and conversion-optimization software, this tool enables users to build opt-in campaigns and test marketing strategies in real time.

- Sendinblue (www.sendinblue.com/): This digital marketing suite automation tool helps users engage their audience, generate leads, and plan out marketing campaigns.
- Xero (www.xero.com/us/): This tool helps minimize business accounting requirements by generating automated invoices, scheduling payments, and organizing important financial documents.

I highly recommend both trying out the automation tools listed here, as well as checking out some other options that pique your interest. The pace at which new automation tools are being launched into the market today is mindboggling. You may find a new tool that completely transforms your side hustle.

Automation and Freelancing: An Unlikely Duo

Freelancing is, at its core, an active form of income. It requires trading time for money. For a freelancing client to be content with the service provided, the freelancer must devote X number of hours to completing the required project. This is how I thought, admittedly, during my first five years in freelancing.

And then I started to wake up. I started to ask myself: why couldn't something like freelancing be automated to some extent? Why couldn't I shave down my workable hours while keeping my earnings constant?

It was this consideration that led me on my automation journey outlined earlier. Sites like Fiverr, after all, are automation tools. Clients can view my gigs, book an order, leave reviews, and spend money on my services while I sleep at night. If I choose to open profiles on multiple freelancing platforms, I can triple this form of lead aggregation. And it's all free!

Pairing simple tools like Slack, an email marketing tool, Loom, Notion, Grammarly (for the writers), Zapier, and Calendly is all you need to integrate other individuals into your freelancing agency. Virtual assistants can oversee every single one of these automated tools, while an overarching agency manager or assistant of some kind ensures that the virtual assistants are following along with their assignments. That leaves just you, the single point of contact, with your assistant while the entire operation hums along below you.

Many of these automation tools come with free options as well. If you need to upgrade (I try to avoid paying if I can, until I know it's worth it), your total every month may still be well under $100. It's not an expensive investment, yet it can take your freelancing business indefinitely to the next level.

In Chapter 13, let's look at the powerful world of virtual assistants, and why you should not be afraid to lean on these people when scaling your side hustles.

Chapter 12 Key Points

- Automating your side hustle is the most important thing you could be doing right now.
- Automation is the key to stop trading time for money.
- Don't be afraid to test out dozens of different automation tools, finding the ones that are right for your business.
- Automation and freelancing pair together better than you might imagine.

13 Vetting Virtual Assistants

If you're serious about changing your life, you'll find a way.
If you're not, you'll find an excuse.

— Jen Sincero

Virtual assistants (VAs) are still largely underutilized in the world of online business today. I will admit, I didn't fully realize their power or potential when I finally agreed to hire two from the Philippines. I figured they could do some hashtag research for me, sort an email here and there, and maybe keep some documents organized. I was completely underestimating what specialized VAs could be doing in my business.

As Karan Kanwar wrote, the next-generation virtual assistants will be far sexier than Alexa and Siri (Kanwar 2020). He posits that VAs, since they are still humans at the end of the day, will be able to smartly select software tools for automation in businesses, while still having that critical thinking power that's missing in a robot like Siri. VAs take the best automated elements of an Alexa, and they make it human.

Plenty of studies have predicted that by 2025, 50% of knowledge workers will use VAs daily, growing from only 2% in 2019 (Afshar 2021). That's a big jump in a short amount of time.

VAs have proven their worth to me repeatedly. They can come specialized in the specific service you offer or possess helpful skills like certifications in Google Analytics and other search engine optimization (SEO) requirements. VAs can come with a background in copyediting or be able to log into the back end of your website and optimize your web pages. They can research keywords for your blogs, and they can check the readability of one of your articles before you publish it online. If you can dream it, truly, a VA can do it.

Let's say you're gearing up to work with a VA. You're ready to bring them into your operation. How can you be sure they are going to do a thorough job for you, and not possibly put your business at risk? Let's look at how I vet my virtual assistants and greater teammates today.

Step 1: Where to Find VAs and Other Talent

The first part of finding quality VA talent is knowing where they reside. Countless people ask me where I found my VAs. In my case, my social media is prominent enough that it brings my teammates to me. This is one of the advantages of having a social media presence. If people know who you are and what you're trying to do, the right people can find you and message you. I know social media can be scary in a lot of ways, but this kind of digital footprint can make this process much easier for you.

If you don't have a large social media presence, that's perfectly fine. Some of the best places to source quality VAs are inside of online community spaces. This includes Facebook groups, LinkedIn groups, Quora boards, Discord channels, and Slack channels. It's free to access most of these groups, and they tend to be highly niched and active communities. Posting about needing VAs in a specifically curated community can put you in contact with some of the most quality people. I believe this is way more effective than anonymous job postings on sites like Indeed.com. (I have heard people have had success on there as well—I just believe specializing your outreach can help you sift through potentially bad candidates.)

Don't forget, you can also find these individuals on freelancing platforms. If you use Fiverr to find your VAs, filter for the specific experience level you want (Fiverr ranks freelancers based on how long they have been on the site and their reviews); then message some potential candidates. Look over their work and send them specific instructions inside of Fiverr that you can test for them to follow. If they don't follow the instructions, you can move onto the next person. There are thousands of quality VAs on these sites right now.

When I am hiring freelancers and VAs, I post to my Instagram Stories with very specific instructions on how to apply. This is my first round of weeding out those who follow instructions, versus those who do not. I specifically tell the applicants how to apply, what to type into the email subject line, and what to attach to the email (for freelancers, I ask for past writing samples; for VAs, I ask for past client references I can call to ask about their performance). If they cannot satisfy this part of the application process, I throw the application out.

Following directions is a huge part of functioning inside of a side hustle and freelancing business model.

For the candidates who make it past this round, I then spend time looking over their portfolios and past work.

Step 2: Portfolio > Resume

The concept of portfolios carrying more weight than resumes is one of my favorite facets of the gig economy. Resumes are outdated, and I am going to be honest, it makes me incredibly happy. Resumes are stuffed with information about degrees, honor societies, and skill sets that the candidate believes they have. They are completely irrelevant in judging a person's ability to satisfy the requirements. When I was hiring my first freelance writer in 2019, I noticed the candidates with more extensive education tended to fall short in the time and work demands. The candidates with "lesser" qualifications surprised me. It made me realize the pretentious structure of resumes has probably prevented the actual best talent of the last decade from achieving the jobs they applied for. Not to mention, resumes favor individuals who had the money to go to college—not everyone has the time or money for that, especially today.

Portfolios, on the other hand, are direct windows into the person and what they can do. Portfolios not only show their past projects, but they are also indicative of how much time they put into formatting the portfolio. Was the portfolio edited and laid out in an aesthetically pleasing way? Were there typos? Can I tell this person put a lot of time into making a gorgeous portfolio?

After I review the branding effort, I start to review the work contained in it. I check for consistency, accuracy, creativity, and thoroughness. If I like what I see with the portfolio, it's time for the final test: putting the candidate to work in real time. Portfolios are certainly more transparent than resumes, but nothing compares to observing the candidate under a specified timeline.

Step 3: Testing Candidates in Real Time

Timeliness, especially in the world of freelancing where orders come with timers, is critically important in a VA and other virtual team members. If I tell a person an order or task is due by a certain time and day, they must meet that deadline. I would rather they ask me a hundred questions over three days than deliver a project late. Therefore, when I test these candidates, one of the major things I am observing is their ability to respond back to me quickly and deliver ahead of time. Since this is obviously a test they are taking to get the job, I want to see a yearning and hunger to get the job. I purposely give them more time than they need, around three to four days, to see if they get the job done in 24 hours. If the candidate does deliver on time, but takes all three days, I don't necessarily count them out. But I do mentally file them behind the candidates who got the work done swiftly. Procrastination has no place in the world of freelancing, which is why I want candidates to demonstrate to me immediately that they are on top of their time management.

Note: When I test my potential freelance writers, I give them actual live Fiverr orders. I will assign one Fiverr order to the 10 candidates. I compare their work and typically, one of them is satisfactory enough to deliver on Fiverr. I do pay my freelance and VA candidates for their work, even if they don't get the position. This is up to your discretion.

If you want to take the testing one step further, you can request a few references from your VAs. Feel free to contact them and ask about the VAs' performance.

After you have taken all these steps, your candidate pool may very well go from 20 to two. That's perfectly fine—you want the quality candidates to become glaringly apparent. One or two quality VAs are more valuable than 10 disorganized VAs.

As we wrap up Part II of this book, we have one more very important chapter to tackle: building out your entire virtual team. I have mentioned how mine is structured in depth thus far, but in the following chapter I am going to neatly organize the structure and explain how you can replicate it for your own business. There is no one right way to build your virtual team, but there are certainly best practices that can make the experience relatively pain-free.

Chapter 13 Key Points

- VAs can take any virtual business to the next level.
- Quality VAs are worth their weight in gold; don't worry about quantity.
- Online niched community spaces like Facebook groups are a great place to source your VAs.
- Develop a testing process to weed out those who can't manage their time and who perform sloppy work.

14 Building Out Your Virtual Team

Stop underestimating what you are actually capable of doing.

— Julie Stoian

It's time to bring together everything we have covered in this part of the book in one hell of an empowered chapter. Your virtual team is the foundation of your business. It's going to be the engine that makes all your wildest dreams a reality. You can't do it without these people, which is why embracing their expertise, support, and camaraderie early on can completely transform your side-hustling quest.

Not to mention that these people will become your friends, confidants, and mentors. They will become a business family in a way, and they will make the entire journey worth it. What is life, really, without the people in it? Making money, growing business systems, and leveraging social media can be exciting, sure, but what's the point of it all at the end of the day if your goal isn't in some way to help other people, inspire them, educate them, and take them under your wing? You will notice on your side-hustling journey that it's these very side effects that, more than anything, make it all worth it. The people make it all addicting. Having that kind of healthy relationship with coworkers that rarely—if ever—existed in an office setting is beyond rewarding. Not being pitted against each other to satisfy quarterly corporate stats is a much healthier relationship for us as human beings.

I care deeply about every single member of my virtual team. My assistant is first and foremost my best friend from when we were little. I trust her with my life and have truly loved watching her grow as a businesswoman. My writers are a group of talented and efficient young people, some with children, who are working hard at freelance writing to achieve financial freedom and provide for their families. My VAs (virtual assistants) are two focused women in the Philippines who can provide a comfortable standard of living for their families by working with American clients. It's really a beautiful thing.

When you pursue financial freedom, you create jobs. It's one of the most valuable things you can do as a member of society. Your side hustle quest can change dozens of people's lives along the way. The ripple effect of side hustling is not only the wealth and money, but also the mindset, inspiration, and experience.

As you can tell, talking about my virtual team makes me emotional (a rare occurrence for me, if you ask the people in my life). I want you to have that, too. Let's look at how mine is structured today.

How I Structure My Virtual Team

My virtual team model is by no means the only model for you to consider today. It's one that I have intuitively built based on different demands of my business. It also takes into consideration the importance of social media content production and influencing as part of my model. I did not have this model strategized when I set out on this journey—I didn't even imagine I'd have a team by the end of it all. I merely pay attention to my business, what it needs, and where it's going. Here is the team structure I have created to make my daily time demands as minimal and flexible as possible:

- **One Agency Manager:** This is the most important role of my entire business model. This is the person who functions, in essence, as me, if I am not able to answer my phone or email for a week or two. When I came down with COVID-19 last year (not fun), my agency manager managed the entire business for me. It was a huge relief since I was unable to work for two solid weeks. I was losing my mind! My agency manager spends most of her time running my freelancing agency, which consists of logging into my Fiverr account and assigning out work to the freelance writers. She also manages my email inbox, assigns writing orders from private clients, and functions as a bookkeeper. There is some pressure with this role, so before you add it to your structure, think long and hard about how you want to vet for this kind of person. Once you find them, your business will be invincible in a way. Note: you do not need to worry about finding this person for your first few years in business.

- **Two VAs:** For now, I work with two VAs in my business. They have Notion documents and Looms from me they can review to do their work every day. Some of their major roles are letting people into my Facebook group, collecting and sorting emails into Flodesk, and reaching out to potential PR clients on sites like LinkedIn. They also proof blogs, upload blogs, help with keyword research, and do SEO research. I do plan to add one or two more VAs this year to support my agency manager in her work every day.

- **Six Freelance Writers:** For years, I had just one freelance writer. Now, I am up to six incredible writers who can take work anywhere from just four hours per week, to my writers who want six hours of work per day. I work with their schedules and expertise. Some writers are better with press releases, while others excel at ebooks. My agency manager works with these writers closely and alerts me to anything I should know.

- **One Video Editor:** My video editor edits all my YouTube videos and podcast videos. He also creates my YouTube thumbnails and turns my podcast videos into three to four 30-second clips I can post to Instagram Reels. He is based in Brazil, and I have enjoyed getting to know him.

- **One Email Marketer:** My email marketer creates lead lists, email templates, and outreach plans for different email marketing campaigns. He works with my agency manager and is based in India.

- **One Podcast Editor:** My podcast editor takes my podcasts and edits the audio so it is crisp and clear for uploading.

- **One Website Builder:** My website builder works with me every year to help me launch typically two to three new websites, while keeping my main alexfasulo.com updated and current. He is based in Denmark.

All these individuals are hired and paid as freelancers. None of them are my employees. They are free to accept or reject jobs and take on other work. I use certain team members, like my website builder, only as I need his support. I may not talk to him for a few months at a time. By working with them in a freelancing arrangement, I do not need to guarantee X amount of work or hours. This arrangement makes it much easier to run an agile operation as the sole proprietor.

The Hub-and-Spoke Model

My virtual business model in the previous section can be described as a hub-and-spoke model. The hub, which is me, sits in the middle of the entire business, while the spokes are attached to me and accessed as needed. I consider them to be part of my business team, yet they function as their own stand-alone freelancers as well. I lean heavily on certain spokes at certain times, and other spokes at other times. This allows me to be as agile and flexible as I want with my business, responding to market changes and demands as they come.

This is one of the major reasons why big businesses or commercially structured entities fail in business. They must commit to a specific loan, inventory, and therefore, employee structure to make it happen. If the industry changes and their product is no longer viable, they end up filing for bankruptcy since their unsold stock and fired employees come with a slew of costs and fees.

With a hub-and-spoke model, you can choose to be a hub with just one spoke. Or you could have 100 spokes. It's completely up to you at any given in time in business. You may go into one year with 50 spokes and emerge with just five spokes since automation tools are replacing the need to hire freelancers. The flexibility of this business model, I believe, is what has made me successful and able to manage 10+ side hustles at any given time.

The Business of One

You are, in essence, a business of one. As just one person, you can do all the things I have listed thus far in this book. You can rely on help and teammates as needed, but at the end of the day, the business belongs to you and no one else. This mitigates the risk associated with having to bring on business partners, stakeholders, and investors. It's just you, out here in the great side-hustling unknown, making the experience anything you want it to be. It's just you, living your life truly the way it was meant to be lived.

The business of one is a very, very new concept in the scope of history. Such a thing could never exist without the technology and automation available to us today. Although technology and social media have introduced new problems into our world (I speak very realistically about the invaluable reach of social media, as well as its detrimental effects on our mental health if not used cautiously), it has made the present era a golden age for the entrepreneurs and side hustlers of the world. I wholeheartedly believe that every single person on the planet has, in some capacity, a little entrepreneurialism in them.

It's for that very reason why, next, I want to talk to you about personal branding and building an online community around you, your personality, and your business of one. Every person has a story to tell, and there is a collection of people online who want to hear your story. Never in a million years could I have imagined that people wanted to hear about my Fiverr experience years ago. To think . . . I thought it was boring! Clearly, I was wrong, and watching my story positively impact people across social media is what makes this all worth it.

I want you to feel comfortable sharing your story, too. In Part III, we are going to look at leveraging your side hustling and freelancing success to launch a personal brand, identifying your core brand components, picking the right social media apps for you, creating content, handling online criticism, and finally, going viral. It is my goal to make you comfortable with the idea of carving out a digital personal brand. Your story matters, trust me. See you in Part III.

Chapter 14 Key Points

- Your virtual team makes any business goal or dream possible.

- Following a hub-and-spoke model will make it easy for your business to adjust to market shifts and changes.

- You are a business of one, and with automation, can be just as successful as a massive corporation with hundreds of employees.

- Virtual teams make it easier for you to take time off and live life the way it was meant to be lived.

III Personal Branding

15 Using Your Freelance and Side Hustle Success to Launch a Personal Brand

If people like you, they'll listen to you, but if they trust you, they'll do business with you.

— Zig Ziglar

Caroline Castrillon came right out in *Forbes* and penned the article "Why Personal Branding Is More Important Than Ever" in 2019, famously stating that "whether you know it or not, you have a personal brand" (Castrillon 2019). Her statement rings truer than ever today, as more and more of our world becomes consumed by social media and virtual connection. You, right now while you read this book, have a personal brand that is apparent to people on social media at this very moment, even if you don't try to curate your content or strategize how you post.

With the metaverse looming not too far on the horizon, personal, virtual brands are going to become not only sought after, but also critical for relevance. In a metaverse, NFT-ridden world, whether you like it or not, personal brands are going to be one of the main ways you connect, apply to jobs, network, build communities, and carve out your own personal meta-life.

But before the immersive technology of web3 (a new form of the World Wide Web based on blockchain technology, incorporating elements of immersive technology) comes knocking at our doors, we remain a species enamored with social media. We eat, sleep, and breathe social media, so much so that the average person is estimated to spend 2.5 hours on social media every day (Cummins 2021). Some of us may be in denial about it, while others have embraced it. Whether you make the content, consume the content, or stalk the content, you are impacted by social media daily. That's why the average person has 8.4 social media apps downloaded to their phone (Dean 2021).

Regardless of how you personally feel about social media and its impact on our mental health (I am never pretending that all of this is "good for us"; I am just a highly pragmatic and practical person who realizes it is not going anywhere), existing in the virtual world with an accessible personal brand is the next logical step on your financial freedom journey.

We All Love a Good Story

Since the beginning of humankind, information, experiences, and lore have been passed down through stories. We all love a good story, a narrative that helps us escape our own mundane reality, if only for a moment. We love to hear about heroes and villains, insurmountable odds, mystical and fantastical adventures, and quirky jokes that help us to feel something real.

That primitive characteristic in us has not gone away just because we own smartphones. If someone can feed us a captivating, interesting, or relatable story, we are going to stop and listen. Even better, we are going to follow that person online, hoping to soak up anything else they share.

Once they tell that first story and we decide we like them, something powerful happens: we start to subconsciously trust them. We recognize that the person we are watching took a risk to expose themselves in some way, telling us they are real, authentic, and genuine. We subconsciously come to see them as a more trustworthy individual in that industry than the person who remains anonymous with a blank profile picture and little to no information available about them online. We would much rather spend our time following the person who entertains us along the way, even if at the end of the day, that person might not be who we perceive them to be. We don't care; we want stories and escapes from the present moment.

It's the same reason you turn on Netflix at the end of the day or pick up a book from your favorite author. I am right there with you, trust me. I am also a human being who loves stories and momentary escapes.

It's coming to this realization that will allow you take the current freelancing and side hustling success you are enjoying and turn it into a personal brand. If you understand this psychology behind social media, you will be able to curate an online presence and story that is irresistible to your followers. Better yet, coming at the whole thing from this storytelling lens will allow you to keep intimate details about your life still private. So many people tell me they could "never do what I do because they want to stay private." To that I always reply, where on my social media, blogs, or website do I disclose my personal feelings and emotions, dating life, or address? Nowhere! I have curated a collaborative story about freelancing that viewers feel both entertained by and invited to participate in right alongside me.

This is where you will start the entire personal branding journey. You will kick it off by thinking about your story, the escape you are going to offer online to other people. Every single person has their own personal story. No two are the same, and with billions of people on social media every day, you can be sure that at least a small percentage of those users will find you and your story inspiring and enthralling. You aren't making content for a couple hundred people in your hometown anymore—you are telling your story to the entire world. Although that may sound scary to some people, allow me to explain the benefits.

The Monetary Benefits of a Personal Brand

When I started posting content to social media regularly in 2019, I was testing the waters. I had been afraid for years to post about my Fiverr success, fearing it would attract even more hate than I was already receiving. When I started to finally post regularly in 2019, something amazing happened: my confidence in myself and my story doubled. Getting it all out there in the open separated me from this looming fear that I was going to be "found out" one day. There it was, sitting on my Instagram; there was nothing to hide. I felt free and more empowered than ever to keep telling that story.

Back in 2019, influencing was still very, very new. Occasionally brands would reach out to me and offer free products in exchange for posts. I was happy with that—who doesn't want a free raincoat every now and then? But by 2020, when I really started to home in on my brand as a freelancing mentor, my engagement grew, and so did the monetary compensation. Brands started to reach out offering free products and a $300 payment to go with it. By the end of the year, as my accounts grew, that $300 became $600. Into 2021, my accounts were growing rapidly, and so were the brands that realized influencers were one of the best ways to advertise. Today, brands pay me $5,000 to $10,000 per collaboration, which can include a variety of different posts, videos, and scripts that they approve before I make the content. This most recent month, I made almost $20,000 alone from brand news, partnerships, sponsorships, and influencer collaborations. I consider that to be side hustle income since my personal brand was merely an unplanned side effect of sharing my original intention of being a freelance writer on social media.

TikTok is full of social media influencers who break down their income with immense transparency. There are individuals with 10,000–20,000 Instagram followers making close to $10,000/month (telling me I am still undercharging). You no longer need to have these multimillion-follower counts to rake in big bucks with influencing. The advertisers know that influencing is going to be the number one method of marketing in the metaverse, and they will line right up to work with your personal brand.

Even better, while all the different social media apps compete today, they are rewarding content creators—finally. YouTube pays in AdSense for video views, Instagram has a Reels Bonus that pays out on video views, and TikTok has a Creator Fund that pairs users with brands while paying out for video views. With these same social media accounts, you can put any link you want into your bio section, driving the traffic back to your side hustles and freelancing profiles. Suddenly, one TikTok video creates money for you as an influencer, member of the

Creator Fund, and drives traffic to your bio link. And that is just the start of it.

Many brands will even have me record and edit one video in TikTok, post it there, and then post that same video to Instagram and other platforms. I end up being paid for four different influencer packages using the same video. A domino effect kicks in when you open your personal brand to working with these advertising partners.

The Personal Benefits of a Personal Brand

Life isn't all about the money. The money is just a form of energy that follows what you are doing and how much value you create to help other people. Creating a personal brand on social media is hands down the most rewarding thing I have done throughout my freelancing career. Finally sharing my story with others has resulted in thousands of messages, emails, letters, and testimonials of people telling me their lives have been changed. Honestly showing people who I am, where I come from, and what I have accomplished with income transparency has demonstrated to them what is truly possible. I still cry from the heartfelt messages I receive from people around the world.

By creating a personal brand online, you will allow the opportunities out there to find you. I am only writing this book right now because my literary agent was able to find me through TikTok. Putting yourself out there will make it easier for your destiny to find you, wherever it may be. Living in the shadows of the internet no longer makes sense in a world where we can't go more than five minutes without picking up our smartphones. Although there is nothing we can do to stop this electronic addiction, I do believe we can make a choice to use it for good. And one of those good things is conquering your fears and posting about your story online.

Now, I know that identifying what it is you want to share online can be the hardest part. You don't want to share the intimate details of your life—but guess what? You don't have to. You already have a side hustle, a freelancing profile, or even a desire to make it all happen. That's why you are reading this book! That is enough to build a personal brand. People want to watch you from square one. They want to know which website you choose for your freelancing agency or which side hustle you picked and why. They want to know if any previous side hustles failed for you, and what tips you would give them to avoid your mistakes in the future. They want to know if you're doing all of this from a country where English is not the main language, or if you're doing it all from a van on the road. They want to know every little thing you feel comfortable giving them about your freelancing and side-hustling momentum.

Showing your laptop at a local café, being honest about your business wins and losses, your unexpected accomplishments and letdowns, and everything in between will captivate an audience. It's therapeutic for you and even more beneficial for them as they learn alongside you. Better yet, while you are helping people, that one side hustle you're working so hard to launch can double in income as it garners you a social media following. It's truly a win-win that does not require you to disclose any kind of uncomfortable information. Although there are plenty of influencers who have no problem sharing the intimate details of their life (and there is nothing wrong with that if you want to do this as well), that's not what you are going to have to do as a side hustler. How awesome is that?

Next, we are going to look at identifying your core personal brand components so you can start to really frame this story you are going to tell. No two brands are the same, but you can certainly spend some time categorizing where you fall and what you feel comfortable sharing. Just a little bit of preparation work in this arena can set you up for quick social media growth that is monetizable in just a few weeks (or months).

Chapter 15 Key Points

- Social media users will trust you if you share your side hustling story.
- Building a personal brand will bring both personal and monetary rewards.
- You do not have to disclose personal information to become a person of interest on social media.
- Social media influencing has become an incredibly lucrative industry today.

16 Identifying Your Core Personal Brand Components

You can't use up creativity. The more you use, the more you have.

— Maya Angelou

This is the fun part. It's time to really envision what your personal brand is going to look like. This brand is going to be an extension of you, how people come to see you when they open their social media. You have total control over your brand attributes and the kind of content you are going to post. Therefore, I need you to try and let go of any social media posting fears as we head through this part of the book. You are in control of your personal brand components.

Many people believe social media branding is completely out of their control. They think if they post one video on Instagram, all hell is going to break loose. Which is why it's time for a moment of tough love: if you are terrified of posting to social media, you must ask yourself, is that because you are often judgmental of everyone else who posts to social media? Why are you judgmental of them? What about their posts makes you feel uncomfortable? You already know that psychology and mindset healing is just as much a part of this journey as everything else. Keep these questions in the back of your mind as we continue.

You are the only person in the world who owns your personal brand. Since there is no two of you, there is going to be something alluring about your personal brand. No one will ever be able to copy it. It's going to unequivocally be yours. It's that very selling point that makes visible online brands so potentially lucrative—there is really no competition.

But first, how do you create this enticing personal brand? What steps do you need to take to really carve out your personal brand components? Let's check it out.

Figure Out Who You Are

Sounds easy, yet this can be the hardest step in any business. In order to build a personal brand that reflects your personal and business identity, you need to know who you are and what you want to show. Here are some questions to ask yourself:

- What do I enjoy doing?
- What do I hate doing?
- What motivates me?
- What drains my energy?
- What are my hobbies?
- Do I prefer to entertain, educate, or shock people?
- Am I introverted or extroverted?

If you can't necessarily identify the answers to these questions, you can call on friends, family, and people in your life who know you and your working habits all too well. As you learn more about your personality, what you like, and what you don't like, you will be able to start carving out a niche. Don't be afraid to make this niche as targeted as possible—of the billions of people online, if even .001% of them resonate with your brand, you are going to be in business. The most successful personal brands online are the ones that aren't afraid to be as specific and niched as possible.

What Do You Want to Be Known For?

Your personal brand gives you a chance to make your own narrative. You control the content you put on social media, so what is it that you want to be known for? Do you want be known as the funny, quirky person? Or the person who gives nonstop tough love to followers? Do you want to be known for doing something brand new? You get to pick, probably for the first time in your life.

As you write down what you want to be known for, you will start to uncover traits and attributes that make you unique. You will also start to learn about your short-term and long-term goals. This can help you to really envision what you want this brand to do for you and your business moving forward.

It's worth grabbing a journal to map all this down. A few good exercises include:

- Writing down 10–15 short-term and long-term goals
- Writing down a timeline of 10 years and pairing the goals off with different times
- Writing down reach-goals or dreams that you previously thought to be out of reach

Mapping it all out can help you create the steps you need to follow if you want to make it a reality.

Who Do You Want to Reach?

In order to be successful online, you need to think about your audience. Your content is nothing without the people who consume it. You can't make affiliate marketing, influencer, or ads revenue if people are not clicking on your content.

You want to ponder who you want to attract to your content. Do you want to pique the interest of college students thinking about what they want to do with their lives? Do you want to speak to an older generation that is looking to learn more about innovations? Do you want to be a blogger for moms, or for dads?

By thinking about your audience, this can help you to pick social media sites that make more sense. For example, TikTok and Twitch tend to attract younger people, while Facebook and Instagram attract a more mature audience. If you want to speak to women only, then sites like Pinterest will be a great way to reach out to them. If you want to work with more men, sites like Reddit and YouTube may be a more realistic way to make it happen.

In that same notebook, start to write out your ideal audience member, what they look like, where they work, and what is important to them. Pretend as though this is a real person with a smartphone who is going to engage with your personal brand.

Sum Your Brand Up in 15 Seconds or Less

It's time to write out your elevator pitch. How are you going to market to these ideal audience members? You are going to need to come up with different ways to package what your brand is going to offer them. And you need to be able to do it in just a few seconds. Attention spans are dwindling, which is why taking

60 seconds to explain why someone should follow you on social media just isn't going to cut it anymore.

TikTok is a great place to learn how to squeeze a lot of information down into just 15 seconds. Spend some time on TikTok looking at other people in your niche and pay attention to how they word their videos. You will be surprised: you can say a lot with a little text and time. It all depends on the messaging and delivery.

Note: you are not going to get this perfectly when you first start out. It took me years, in fact, to arrive at my freelancing influencer brand that I have today. I messed around with different messaging and paid close attention to its engagement. Allow your audience to tell you what is, and is not, working with your personal brand. One of the worst things you can do is get stuck in this idea that you are not going to budge on your brand attributes at all. Be willing to be flexible and cater to the people buying your digital products.

Poll Your Audience Weekly

Your personal brand is going to change and evolve as your audience and the industry do. As a result, poll your audience as much as possible. Instagram allows for polling right inside of the Instagram Stories feature. You can also ask questions and allow your followers to submit their responses. The same thing holds true on Facebook pages and inside of Facebook groups. It's an invaluable way to accumulate information about your audience so you can arrive at a personal brand that serves both you and them.

You can start the polling process at any time. Even right now with social media that is not curated to a personal brand, start asking your followers about what they would be more interested in seeing. Maybe you love graphics and design and copywriting equally. Ask your followers the kind of content they would want to see more and observe their answers. If there is a massive demand for copywriting, maybe that is a sign.

When I was starting on TikTok in 2020, I never imagined people would be interested in learning about Fiverr. I thought people would find it incredibly boring. But, as my engagement with Fiverr-focused content increased, I paid attention. There is more to me than freelancing on Fiverr, but it's what the people wanted. So, I embraced it and started creating tons of Fiverr content. I am glad I listened because that Fiverr social media content is the reason you are reading this book today! It does not mean I need to be bound by that brand for the rest of my life. I have the freedom to change and shift it as I see fit. Listening to your audience can have tangible personal and lucrative rewards.

Remember to Be Flexible

After you follow these steps, you should be able to loosely identify a niche or brand that you want to offer to the online world. There is no pressure with what you have chosen—it may very well change. Allow your mind to accept possible change in the future. Be agile with the brand so your audience can feel connected to you.

Don't become too obsessed with the details of this initial brand. Understanding your target audience and a few attributes of your brand is enough to get started. Analysis paralysis can creep in aggressively here if you cling to your brand attributes with an unwillingness to shift or change them. The biggest part of launching anything new online is recognizing that it is not going to be perfect at first—and that's okay.

Next, we are going to get into the technical information of picking the right social media apps for your personal brand. Spreading yourself too thin is a very real problem for people launching personal brands. By understanding these social media communities, you can more strategically pick the right ones in the beginning so you do not experience burnout. With knowledge comes power!

Chapter 16 Key Points

- To create a personal brand, you need to spend time getting to know yourself and your personality traits.
- Plan for your short-term and long-term goals to learn more about what's important to you.
- Poll your audience in order to create a personal brand in conjunction with them.
- Be flexible in your personal brand expectations and growth.

17 Picking the Right Social Media Apps for You

Social media is the ultimate equalizer. It gives a voice and a platform to anyone willing to engage.

— Amy Jo Martin

There are a lot of social media apps in existence today. Perhaps too many. It's the paradox of too many choices again—it can stop you in your tracks before you even get started. That's why I want to help you navigate the social media realm, so that you feel it's more approachable before you convince yourself that this is not for you.

I currently have a presence on five social media apps that I try to update regularly. I put 90% of my focus into just one: TikTok. I then repurpose the content I make on TikTok to Instagram, Pinterest, and YouTube. My presence on Facebook is merely for my closed Facebook groups. In total, I have scaled to these five social media apps because it's easy to repurpose my TikTok videos onto them. Really, I only put original content on Instagram (via Instagram Stories) and TikTok. That's about it.

However, I do not recommend you start out trying to have a presence on five social media apps. It took me years to expand this far and wide. I am a big advocate of starting with just two. Having more than one will give you a chance to engage with different audiences so you can learn about your brand heading into the future. Yet trying to tackle more than two social media apps in the beginning is going to overwhelm you. You want to do everything possible to avoid being overwhelmed so that you can feel confident enough to make this a reality.

I am now going to provide you with a breakdown of the biggest, most trafficked social media apps, their typical users, and their pros and cons.

(Note: The following statistics in the demographic breakdown sections are based on demographics for the United States, specifically.)

Facebook

Recognized as the grandparent of the social media apps in existence today, Facebook still boasts 2.91 billion users (Goldsmith 2021), making it the most downloaded social media app in the world right now. As growth for the app has slowed in recent years due to a shift in social media user preference, Facebook has become a place that is advantageous for growing tight-knit communities, many of which can include a charge for entrance (I own the Freelance Fairyland Marketplace on Facebook, an open freelancing marketplace that requires a $5/month charge to access it).

Demographic Breakdown

- 56% of users are male; 44% are female.
- Largest demographic is users 25 to 35 years old.

Pros

- The best social media app for growing online communities that can be monetized.
- Still the largest social media app in existence, making it one of the best places to run paid ads.
- Great place to target older demographics.

Cons

- Facebook is not being downloaded by younger generations, especially Gen Z today.
- Facebook has an overall serious culture, one that is not receptive to the kind of content you would find on TikTok.

Instagram

Facebook smartly purchased Instagram when it sensed a growing culture of Facebook rejection as more parents and grandparents downloaded the Facebook app. Today, Instagram has close to 1.5 billion daily active users, who jump onto the app to post to Instagram Reels, IGTV, Stories, and Guides. Instagram has become one of the more complex social media apps, which allows users to share many different forms of content as the app struggles to remain "cooler" than apps like TikTok and Twitch.

Demographic Breakdown

- 50.8% of users are female; 49.2% are male.
- Largest demographic is users 25 to 34 years old.

Pros

- Instagram contains a wide variety of demographics, making it easy to curate a community that works with any brand or industry.

- Instagram allows users to share everything from photos and videos, to fleeting stories and longer-form content.
- Instagram's large user base makes it another great place to run ads for brands.

Cons

- As Instagram launches more and more features, the app is becoming confusing to use and is lacking in a centralized brand.
- Natural growth and reach on Instagram is dismal when compared to apps like TikTok.

LinkedIn

Regarded as the professional social media network where business personnel go to upload resumes and testimonials, LinkedIn has held its own over the years. Today, they are toying with launching their very own freelancing marketplace, which is why I recommend everyone get on LinkedIn and update their profile today. LinkedIn has 500 million total users, and offers everything from recruiting, direct messaging, and connecting to LinkedIn articles, which can function as your very own professional blog.

Demographic Breakdown

- 57% of users are male; 43% of users are female
- Largest demographics is users 46 to 55 years old

Pros

- LinkedIn is going to have its own freelancing marketplace.
- Posting blogs to LinkedIn can be a great way to drive traffic to your freelancing business.

- LinkedIn automation makes it easy to send dozens of messages to potential clients on the app every day.

Cons

- LinkedIn has a hard-to-follow interface and can be cumbersome to use all day.
- The spam messages sent on the app can be exhausting.

Pinterest

Pinterest is one of the most concentrated female-dominated social media apps in existence today. If your business caters to women, home décor, decorations, cooking, and accessorizing, Pinterest is going to change your life. At 444 million daily active users, Pinterest now also hosts a Story Pins feature (similar to a TikTok or IG Reel). I use Pinterest Story Pins when I repost my TikToks, and it has effortlessly grown my account to 16,000+ users.

Demographic Breakdown

- 77.1% of users are female; 14.8% are male; 8.4% are unspecified.
- 8/10 moms use Pinterest (Geyser 2021).
- Largest demographic is users 50 to 64 years old (Aslam 2022).

Pros

- Pinterest has some of the best engagement you will find on social media today.
- Since the Pinterest demographic is very unified, you will find quick success with industries that do well on the app.

- The overall Pinterest tone and community are one of positive reception.

Cons

- Pinterest is not as welcoming to non-feminine industries.

TikTok

TikTok is giving everyone a run for their money, with over 1 billion users and counting. The video-only app has done a great job of offering just one form of content posting and sticking with it. TikTok has stated they are considering adding in TikTok Stories and subscriptions, so that users can charge a premium per month to share some of their best content. TikTok remains one of the easiest places to go viral through social media today, which is why I am going to go through all the ins and outs of the app in Chapter 20.

Demographic Breakdown

- 60 percent of users are female; 40 percent are male (Dean 2022a).
- Largest demographic is users 10 to 19 years old.

Pros

- Easiest social media app on which to create viral content today.
- Has an advanced video editing tool so that you can download TikToks and repurpose them to other social media apps.
- Has an overall fun, receptive, and creative atmosphere that is welcoming to new creators.

Cons

- TikTok's flagging system is still faulty and can end up removing videos for no reason (contact TikTok about unfair video removal).
- TikTok does not allow users (presently) to post links inside of their videos.

Twitter

At 436 million users, Twitter has struggled over the last decade to compete with the big dogs. They have carved out their own unique space as one of the most effective apps to make direct contact with reporters and journalists. The app is also experiencing a resurgence today thanks to cryptocurrency and the non-fungible token (NFT) community relying on Twitter as one of their primary apps to connect. The nature of text-only posts make it an intimate place to connect closely with followers and learn more about their sentiments.

Demographic Breakdown

- 63.7% of users are male; 36.3% are female.
- Largest demographic is users 18 to 29 years old.

Pros

- It's easy to make content on Twitter—simply write out a few sentences and click Post.
- Direct messages make it easy to connect with hard-to-reach industry personnel, like journalists.

Cons

- The app has an overall toxic culture with negativity and cyberbullying.
- Twitter has become a highly censoring app that takes down a variety of tweets if they do not like them.
- The app is not as trafficked as it used to be.

Twitch

Twitch is, in a lot of ways, the future where social media is headed. It's a Live-streaming social media app that allows users to video-game, cook, eat, tell stories, and do a variety of other things in real time. The cult-like followings that develop from constant Live content creates a fiercely loyal following that will buy almost anything from the Twitch user. I believe Twitch is a precursor to the kinds of social media apps we will be using in the metaverse.

Demographic Breakdown

- 65% of users are male; 35% are female (Dean 2022b).
- Largest demographic is users 16 to 24 years old.

Pros

- Going Live consistently in the app builds a very committed following that can be easily monetized.
- Live content is the future of social media; the sooner you get used to it, the more successful your brand is going to be.
- You do not need advanced skills to be successful on Twitch; simply eating a meal with the sound turned up can attract a following.

Cons

- Many Twitch users have a suite of advanced production electronics they use to really enhance their Live experience.
- Twitch tends to do the best in the evening hours, making it an app that won't be compatible with morning people.

YouTube

After Google, YouTube is the second-biggest search engine on the internet, and for good reason. The app has become one of the go-to places to learn new things, watch news recaps and podcast videos, and follow creators who document their days in detailed vlogs. With 2.562 billion daily users, YouTube is just barely trailing Facebook as the most downloaded social media app in existence today. With such a large user base, there is a nook for everyone in any industry on YouTube.

Demographic Breakdown

- 62% of users are male; 38% are female.
- Largest demographic is users 18 to 25 years old.

Pros

- YouTube monetization is one of the best payouts available to creators on any social media app.
- YouTubes can go viral months after they are posted, creating sustained revenue for six or more months.
- There is a community for everyone on YouTube.

Cons

- It can require a lot of time and production to make viral-worthy videos on YouTube.

- YouTube SEO, keywords, and so on can overwhelm creators.

Where to Go from Here

With this information, you should be able to identify which social media apps make the most sense for your brand. There are no rules that state you can't switch or test out other apps in the future. I figure that since all these apps are free, why wouldn't you eventually explore what they can do for your personal brand? Their demographics are also ever changing, so bearing that in mind, understand that one year from now your ideal audience could be on an app you had not previously considered.

Next, let's look at the actual content production process and how to automate it. Although there is no way to completely automate a personal brand since the main ingredient is your personal attention, you can create a schedule that works with you and your current businesses.

Chapter 17 Key Points

- Get on two social media apps to start so you are not overwhelmed.
- Recognize that demographics shift; be open to trying out new apps in the future.
- Over time, aim to get on even more social media apps once you feel comfortable with the process.
- For catch-all apps, try Facebook and YouTube; for more niche audiences, try Pinterest and Twitch, and so on.

18 Creating and Automating Content

You don't need a corporation or a marketing company to brand you now: you can do it yourself. You can establish who you are with a social media following.

— Ray Allen

Creating content online is just as much a calculated, research-based endeavor as it is a creative one. You don't have to be the most "creative" person to ever hit planet earth to make content on social media. I find the most successful content creators of all are the ones who perfectly blend the art of research with artistic expression.

The online world is equally receptive to extroverts and introverts. In fact, I find that most of my favorite TikTok creators self-identify as introverts in real life. At the end of the day, making content is a lonely pursuit: it's just you, your phone, and maybe some lights or a mic. You don't need to perform in front of real people. You can find the settings, spaces, and times that make you feel the most comfortable. It can be something that anyone can do, I promise.

Before you automate the content development process, let's first go over how to create it. As I mentioned in Chapter 17, making content on social media is going to be something that you'll change over time. The type of content you make today may not be the content your audience wants from you one year from now. Many trends on TikTok can come and go in just a few weeks. Being timely with what people want and adjusting your posting style can really help you grow a following that makes your personal brand highly sought-after. People can tell when you are personally present on your social media; they want to follow someone who they believe is passionate about their virtual community.

So, where do you start? How do people make their first social media post? What should it look like? These are the questions that stop people in their tracks. Don't worry, I have you covered. Let's look at some of easiest ways to start churning out social media content.

Six Social Media Post Ideas You Can Use Today

As you embark on your social media content-curating journey, here are some ideas to inspire you and get you on track:

1. **Reposting the news:** We can't look away from news headlines, whether we want to admit it or not. Sharing news articles and statistics from your industry can be a great conversation starter. You can repost them to your Instagram Stories, or make entire videos commenting on them. You can agree or disagree with the news. Since news commentary is often based on emotion, this can be a great way to get natural engagement and comments on your posts.

2. **Repost user-generated content:** When your followers start to tag you, your business, or your products, always repost it.

Share it to your different social media profiles. This provides social media to your other followers and shows that you are trustworthy.

3. **Create an inside joke with your followers:** Come up with something clever that only the "true members" of your community will get. Maybe you can document a time when you completely failed at the business that day. Invent a made-up word you use to refer to that day. Document the whole day on Instagram and really allow your followers to feel like they have an inside joke with you. Carry it over for months after.

4. **Offer giveaways:** Giving away things for free in the beginning can be a great way to get your posts moving. Require followers to follow your other accounts and sign up for your newsletter, etc. to receive the freebie. Encourage them to post and tag you when they do, so that you can use this user-generated content on your accounts.

5. **Engage with polls and questions:** Post polls and questions to your followers daily. This will get them to engage your profile and give you responses that you can then use to make additional content. If you, for example, ask your followers what they are most looking forward to at the holidays, you can do a response video/photo with their answer. It's a great way to keep the flow of content going while also being an effective way for you to conduct your own research.

6. **Go Live:** Going Live is one of the best ways to boost your profiles in the algorithm. It may be uncomfortable at first, but it will be worth it when your accounts start to grow and you develop public speaking skills along the way. I go Live on TikTok three to four times per week, as well as Instagram three to four times per month.

Which Kinds of Social Media Posts Do the Best?

Right now, social media is in the era of video. Videos perform infinitely better over plain text and photo posts. People want an authentic experience from you. They feel that video is something that exposes creators, so they can't hide behind lies and Photoshop. Any kind of video will perform decently well from Pinterest to YouTube.

That's why you want to build a social media strategy around making video content. Here is how I do mine:

- I spend two to three hours one day per week recording 10 to 20 TikToks. I then edit them and save them as drafts.
- When I post the TikTok, I download the video through TikSave (removes the watermark).
- I post that same video to Pinterest Story Pins, Instagram Reels, and YouTube Shorts, following each app's unique posting requirements.
- If I feel the video is exceptional, I elect to post the Instagram Reel to my grid, otherwise known as your profile. I spend time writing a compelling caption of 150–200 words in the notes pad on my phone.

This requires about five to six hours of my time every week. The payoff far exceeds the time that went into it. As you spend more time making content, you will come to like it. It will become a creative outlet that allows you to feel expressive and connected to people who love what you are doing.

Posting and Algorithmic Hacks

No single person has the algorithms of these sites figured out. They purposely do not tell you how to hack their algorithms. But as someone who has been very aggressively posting to social media for years now, I have noticed some trends:

- Going Live consistently for four to five days in a row kick-starts new followers to your account. These sites reward you for going Live and making their app worth other users' time. The longer they can keep people on these apps, the more money they make.

- Responding to comments from your followers is important, no matter how big you are. Giving them hope that you may personally engage them will keep them intrigued and coming back for more.

- Worrying about what time you post is not as important as the content itself. If the content is authentic and alluring, it will hit the algorithmic airwaves. Don't get caught up in the details.

- Account warnings will drop you out of the algorithm. If you think a topic is going to get you an account warning, consider the risk if you are making good money through that social media app.

Automating Your Content

You already know I am looking at ways to automate content creation and posting. I do want to reiterate that there is no way to completely automate creating content and engaging your audience. You do have to trade some time being present during a social media Live video and in the comment section. Your followers will know if you are not.

Still, here are some of my favorite automation tools I use when posting both social media and regular online content:

- **Buffer** (Buffer.com): Create content, schedule it, and automatically post it through the Buffer dashboard. Track analytics on your posts to tailor your future content creation.

- **Hootsuite** (Hootsuite.com): Hootsuite was my best friend when I managed social media accounts. It has a simple interface where you can manage multiple social media accounts at once, schedule content, and post it.

- **Hopperhq** (Hopperhq.com): Visualize your Instagram grid before you post to it. Move around different pieces of content to arrive at the visual brand your desire.

- **Otter.ai** (Otter.ai): This is one of my favorite AI tools to use today. It takes audio recordings, like my podcasts, and transcribes them into blogs. I then have my VAs edit the blogs and post them to my website.

- **Pallyy** (Pallyy.com): This social media platform helps people manage visual content campaigns with an aesthetic interface.

- **SocialPilot** (SocialPilot.co): This social media automation and analytics tool helps with calendar and client management, making it a great solution for freelancers who create content as part of their service offering.

These are the automation tools I have personally used to date. All of them have been helpful and worth their subscription fees. There are countless other social media automation platforms I have not personally tried that may be worth your time. As always, proceed with caution and take time to read the software reviews.

At this point, your social media is present, your online personal brand is growing, and people are interested. You have your supporters, which means that you also have your internet "haters." There is no way to make content online and not have them. In the next chapter, we are going to look at hater expectations, how to handle them, and how to rewire your brain to withstand any amount of internet anger.

Chapter 18 Key Points

- Start with simple social media content posts so you do not overwhelm yourself.

- Reposting user-generated content, news articles, and poll responses is a great way to engage your audience.

- Although you can't automate every element of social media posting, it's worth onboarding a few different automation tools to make your life easier.

- Have fun with the process and embrace your newfound online communities.

19 Handling Online Criticism and Hate

Content is fire. Social media is gasoline.

— Jay Baer

Where there are people, there is going to be envy. It's been happening since the beginning of humankind. Many of the oldest tales passed down by generations revolve around envy among rulers, nations, and even family. It's a natural human emotion that all of us can't help but experience from time to time.

The internet is a double-edged sword. It can change your life, set you financially free, and change people's lives around the world. But it can also inspire a slew of negative and toxic responses out of users who allow their envy and insecurity to swallow them whole. And to my knowledge, there is nothing we can do about this sector of people online today.

Rather than wish they would disappear, I believe it's best to anticipate their behavior and hate. They are going to show up on your posts the moment you start driving momentum to your personal brand. Where there is growing security and confidence, there is also that one internet user who is determined to lob their hate and trauma onto you.

We're not wired as humans to be exposed to the personal feelings and opinions of so many people. That's why you need to carefully craft how much time you do, and do not, spend on social media, as well as how much time you spend reading unhappy comments and direct messages. There is a happy medium that can be established here, and it's taken me a few years to perfect it. But with these methods, I believe you can embark on a virtual journey that does not have to end in feeling overwhelmed by internet haters.

Step 1: Anticipating the Hate

I know people who try and pick the "least controversial" social media topic they can possibly find in order to avoid hate. They would rather change their passions and interests in order to appease the small sector of people who are going to hate on anything they can find. I did this my first few years on social media. I hid my entire business and freelancing life from social media because I knew in my heart it would ruffle some feathers. When my story came out anyway in 2018, my biggest fear came true: internet haters started to tell me I was a liar. This was hard to stomach at first, but then something incredible happened. I started to develop confidence because following my biggest social media fear coming true, I had survived. Not only had I survived, but I also started to learn about the thousands of people around the world who had been positively impacted by my story.

I always say, for one angry internet hater, there are 10 internet supporters rooting for you. They're just too busy building their own empires to flood your content with supportive comments every day.

When you give a person with an unhappy situation a phone where they can comment whatever they want with no repercussions, they are going to take it. Accepting this as inescapable will make it much less shocking when it happens. And when it does happen and you're still breathing on the other side, you will realize the fear of experiencing internet hate was silly. Your content is going to change lives, making all of this beyond worth it.

Step 2: Filtering the Hate

Let's say your social media profiles have a few thousand followers at this point. You've experienced your first few hate comments and emails. Maybe people are starting to send you toxic direct messages they hope hurt you. It's time to put a filter into place to protect yourself and your own mental health.

In 2021, CNBC ran an episode on my life and the money I have made as a freelancer. The video went intensely viral, impacting people around the world. Although tens of thousands poured in thanking me for sharing my story, I experienced the most internet hate I had ever dealt with thus far in my life. It was scary, I am not going to lie. The hate comments were more than I could filter. People started writing articles stating I am a liar. It was overwhelming.

It forced me to put a filter in place. Here are the three steps I took to protect my mental space going forward:

1. I stopped reading all direct messages on all social media sites. I no longer open them.

2. I hired my best friend to be a buffer between me and these messages and emails. You can hire anyone to manage your email for you and filter out the hate emails. This way, you aren't even aware they dropped into the inbox that day.

3. I limited the time I spent on social media after posting my content. I still spend time going live, answering supporters, and posting, don't get me wrong. But then I get off the app before I start going down the rabbit hole and reading hate comments on videos from three months ago. It's just not worth it.

Virtual assistants (VAs) are excellent options for filtering hate comments. You can have them review your direct messages and alert you to the valuable ones in a form they compile outside of the app. You can also have them personally manage and sort your emails for you, after they throw out the hate ones. In this scenario, don't be afraid to ask for help (see Chapters 13 and 14 for finding and vetting VAs).

Step 3: Learning to Love Your Haters

I am going to get psychological on you all right now. Your haters, in many ways, are some of your biggest supporters. They are the ones engaging your content, sharing it to their friends, and downloading it to obsess over. These activities on your profile boost your ranking in the algorithm. Better yet, many of these haters are buying your products, books, and courses to prove to themselves that they are "right" about how they feel about you.

They are, in essence, infatuated with you. I am not saying this is a healthy phenomenon, but it is one that is going to massively grow your accounts. Cardi B famously thanked her haters after accepting an award, stating that they are the ones that go ahead and download her music first. She's not wrong. Kim Kardashian has echoed that sentiment, thanking her haters for posting her product links far and wide across the internet.

At the end of the day, these people are in bad places. They are not happy with their lives. They have probably had a series of traumatic things happen to them, and they are not sure how to fix their current reality. They are throwing hate at you to soothe their wounded soul. The hate is not about you as an individual; it's a projection from their insecurity. You just happen to be the trigger. When you realize it's not as personal as you think, you will be able to mentally separate yourself from the hate you receive online.

The more hate you weather, the more it loses its power over you. The haters will come and go—but they will be your biggest marketing department if you learn to love them over time. Say a prayer that they find some healing and go on with your day. Don't let this fear of hate stop you from transforming your life. Once I got over this fear, I realized I should have done it sooner. Being your true and authentic self online will attract your tribe. People who genuinely like you and what you stand for will appear, because you had the courage to put yourself out there. I have made some of the best friends and mentors of my life by just being myself online.

Now that we have the psychology behind online hate out of the way, it's time to talk about the most powerful social media app at your disposal today. TikTok singlehandedly changed my entire life online, introducing me to every person I work with today. The natural reach on TikTok is so much greater than Instagram or Facebook that I cannot promote it enough. In the next chapter, I will go over how I have used TikTok specifically to grow my personal brand, change lives, and make a handsome living while doing it. I am urging you to see the app as more than just a place where teens are dancing.

Chapter 19 Key Points

- Online hate is inevitable if you post your story on social media today.
- Anticipating hate will make it less shocking when it happens.
- Take steps to filter out hate for your own mental health.
- Learn to love your haters—they are secretly your biggest supporters.

20 TikTok Goes the Clock

Too many brands treat social media as a one-way, broadcast channel, rather than a two-way dialogue through which emotional storytelling can be transferred.

— Simon Mainwaring

There is one social media app that I believe outshines all the rest today. This one app provides more reach, connection, and exposure than all of them combined, or at least that has been my experience. That's why I feel TikTok deserves its very own chapter—it's really the one app you need to download to kick-start this entire journey.

Over one billion people use TikTok every single day (Dean 2022). When compared to Instagram, which is nearing 1.4 billion users, it's worth considering that TikTok is much younger—only founded in 2016. Instagram has been around since 2010. That is why my pundits believe that TikTok is going to surpass Instagram soon as the most downloaded app of all time.

Why are so many people rushing to download the music-based video-only social media app? TikTok does something that the other social media sites don't do—it requires creators to be purely and unequivocally honest. It's a social media app that exposes those who were previously hiding or lying about their identity. As an app that places emphasis on real-time video caught and edited right inside of their editor tool, TikTok is almost the antithesis of Instagram. Users can't hide behind filters and Photoshop. What you see is what you get.

That's why TikTok users trust their favorite creators with a fierce loyalty—they feel that they really know them. They know that in a video, it's impossible to Photoshop your body or change the skin on your face. Users know that creators can't pull a fast one on them anymore, forcing them to be more human-like. It's finally a social media experience where we don't get on there and feel bad about ourselves. I notice when I get off TikTok, it's the one social media app that put me in a better mood before I got on it.

There are several major benefits found on TikTok that you cannot find on another social media app today.

Fierce Loyalty and a Forgiving Algorithm

The TikTok algorithm is the most advanced algorithm in the game today. It's so advanced that it will feed you content that is creepily in line with your personal interests. TikTok was even able to figure out I love music festivals before I had ever posted or commented on a music festival video.

This algorithm is also a forgiving one. Your exposure on TikTok is so much farther and wider than it is on Instagram.

Instagram is a tough nut to crack. With TikTok, you can post a random 15 different videos and have a good chance that one of them will go viral. TikTok wants your content to go viral—it keeps users on their app. They are working alongside you to grow your profile. My TikTok impressions are millions more than my Instagram every month—even though I post the same content to both.

What's also fun about this algorithm is that you don't have to niche it so intensely. Each time you post to TikTok, the algorithm recognizes your video as its own unique piece of content. You can post five videos back to back and have an equal chance that every single one will go viral. The stuffiness and rules of Instagram don't apply. Think it, film it, and post it. Sit back and see what happens.

This is what I did in 2020. My first viral video connected me with new friends, business partners, and plenty of ebook sales. Since the viral video was one that showed my personality, people started to follow me. I gained 100,000 followers in just three months. These were loyal followers, too. They trusted me, so they went ahead and purchased my products. By October 2020, I had my bio link changed to my new online courses I filmed with my course partner, who, of course, found me on TikTok. By January 2021, these courses were making close to $40,000/month. We went on to have 100,000+ course sale months in the spring of 2021 when my CNBC video went viral.

Loyal followers will gladly check out your products. They already trust you. You're not just some anonymous ad in their Facebook feed. They know you, they like it, and they are willing to view whatever it is that you are selling. This trust is so invaluable that you can go ahead and sell 10 more books and

20 more courses over the next few years, and these followers will probably buy all of them. That's the amazing connection that's built on TikTok between creators and users.

Gen Z's "Come as You Are" Comfort

TikTok is what I like to call a Gen Z app. I am a millennial, but only two years away from the Gen Z cut-off. I see myself as a person who embodies a little bit of both generations. TikTok is a Gen Z playground, which is a great thing in the world of social media. For all the assumptions older generations make about Gen Z, they have created a much more welcoming and healthier social media atmosphere. Allow me to explain.

Gen Z rejects the Photoshop idea of perfectionism on Instagram. They are the authentic social media users that get on there every day and show the acne on their face without makeup. They create dancing videos in sweatpants. They openly post about trauma and mental health with their followers. They are shockingly transparent, to the point where older generations comment on their lack of "class." They are always on the lookout for bullies in the comment sections, ready to dive in and defend someone who needs it.

I find it wildly refreshing. It's a no-pressure app. Whereas on Instagram there is a pressure to look and act a certain way, on TikTok all bets are off. Post whatever you want, whenever you want. Pay attention to what does well. Make more of that content, choose music to go with it, and allow your imagination to run wild. You can be your true self on TikTok, no matter how weird that might be. Individuality and genuine transparency are praised on the app, and I find it incredibly comforting.

If this personal brand and social media journey sounds scary to you, apps like TikTok are a great place to get started.

The Odds Are in Your Favor

Rumor has it that TikTok hands one viral video over to every new creator within their first 10 to 20 videos. This was my experience. My first videos flopped, but all of a sudden, a random video I had edited in the app (probably my tenth video) hit the viral interwaves. It blew up to over two million views in about four weeks. This one video grew my account close to 80,000 followers and created about $4,000 in ebook revenue.

Today, with an entire online course suite, if I have one viral video that goes anywhere from two to four million views, I receive about 100,000–200,000 new followers and close to 100,000 in course sales. It's a no-brainer, to say the least.

I have seen the most bizarre and typically not-viralworthy accounts blow up on TikTok. I have seen videos of people who talk about the monsters in the Appalachian Mountains they don't teach us about in school (I love creepy stuff), people who do videos on histories of lakes around the world, and even people who get on the app sitting in their backyard talking about their day and what they learned from the people in their lives. You don't need to be a model, mega rich, a traveler, or someone with an insane story. Coming as you are is enough for TikTok. In fact, it's praised, and it's certainly an accepting place that will make everyone feel comfortable creating content.

Of all the social media apps at your disposal, I can't recommend TikTok enough. I believe it's where you should start your personal brand journey. I know it can all seem overwhelming, but if you spend a few days on TikTok watching the videos and playing around with the video-editing tool, it will start to come together.

Before we finish off Part III of this book, I want to touch on one more topic: virality. In the next chapter, we will go over the concept of going viral, how to increase your chances of going viral, and finally, how to capture monetary reward from when you do go viral. Virality should be the end goal for every person creating content online today.

Chapter 20 Key Points

- The authentic nature of TikToks will inspire a fierce loyalty in your following.
- TikTok has a much more forgiving algorithm that gives everyone a chance to go viral.
- Gen Z has created a very comforting and welcoming atmosphere for new creators on TikTok.
- Just one viral video can make you tens of thousands of dollars on TikTok.

21 A Crash Course on Virality

Social media is here. It's not going away; not a passing fad.
Be where your customers are: in social media.

— Lori Ruff

Everyone wants to go viral. Having one video take off into the farthest corners of the internet can make you some serious money—and quickly. That's the number one concern I see in messages to me about social media content: "How long until I go viral and my accounts blow up?"

If we could all crack the code on virality every day, the internet would be a different place. Not every video can go viral. It would saturate the content that deserves to be viral. Too many people blame algorithms and technical aspects, as opposed to looking at the actual value of their content. Videos that are viral-worthy will go viral. It's the Law of Virality, as I like to call it. Videos that were made in a totally unique, captivating, shocking, and creative process will find their way to the social media users who want to see them. You do not have to worry about doing anything special once you post the video to make this happen. Step back, put the phone down, and see how your audience responds.

That's why going viral is just as much the value of the content as it is your audience. Although you may have tons of ideas for the content you want to create, you must be paying attention to its reception with your audience. Going viral is a research game— the more time you spend studying the videos that go viral in your niche, the more you will come to understand the psychology behind why they went viral. In case you can't tell at this point, I am a research nut. It's how I launched a Fiverr business that acquired clients quickly. I sat behind my computer and studied my competitors for hours. Going viral is no different.

Before you come up with the viral video concept, you need to first do your homework.

Conducting Viral Research

"If it's not broke, don't fix it." My very first viral video was a copy of a trend on TikTok. I didn't directly copy someone else or plagiarize. But I did take the concept and the song used in the trend, and then I applied it to my unique situation with my own video clips. I had seen the video perform well for other creators, so I adapted it for my brand. Boom. It went viral.

Now, I didn't just happen upon this viral trend with luck. I had spent days searching different terms on TikTok like "freelance," "side hustles," and "digital nomads." I then combed over the videos that were doing the best in each category. I still do this today, even with the following I have. Social media is an ever-changing landscape, which is why falling in love with researching will be key if you want to consistently earn big bucks at content creation.

Let's use the example of a TikTok account that shows people how to make money at dropshipping. You would go to the TikTok search bar and type in terms like "dropshipping," "ecommerce," and "making money online." Start there and see what videos pop up at the top. Click on them and then look at the hashtags they used. They may have used hashtags you never thought up for your niche. Study the first videos and then click on these new hashtags and repeat the process. Not only will you learn about new hashtags to use, but you will also stumble upon a variety of viral videos that will really help you envision the video(s) you want to create.

This process holds the same on any social media app. On Instagram, search the different Reels that are trending. Scroll through your Reels feed and see which videos are doing well with engagement. You can save these videos on any app so you can go ahead and use the same song in your video. Using trending songs is a great tactic for going viral—if the song is trending, that means it's something current social media users want to be hearing that day.

You can never do too much research in the art of virality. You just need to make sure you don't allow the research to give you analysis paralysis. At some point, you must start making the content.

Creating Viral-Worthy Content

If I could tell you a catch-all secret of how to make content that goes viral every single time, I would. But that's the very concept of virality in a nutshell—you can't always know what is and is not going to go viral. Based on the research you are going to do ahead of time, you can have an idea of what's really sticking at that time. Or you can go totally rogue and try out a brand-new concept. It's harder to go viral this way, but if you end up creating a trend from your initial video, the virality potential from this is unmatched.

From studying my past viral videos, here are common attributes I notice in the content:

- **Controversy:** I am not saying you need to go on social media and make an insane political statement to get everyone fighting. But you do need to have something in the video that can cause commenters to engage one another. Be careful not to become someone who makes clickbait content constantly—your followers will stop trusting you. One example of a recent controversial video of mine is when I stated that I have 10 different streams of income, thereby helping me to "break out of the matrix." Not only did the 10 streams of income get people worked up, but the breaking out of the matrix statement had people either in complete agreement or disagreement. I posted that video months ago, and people are still commenting under it.

- **Front-facing, talking:** People want to connect with people online today. They want to see you, up close, and hear your voice. They want you to talk to the camera and proclaim something or teach it. My most viral videos are always the ones in which I talk. This creates an immediate connection as opposed to video clips that are accompanied by a song and some text bites. These kinds of voiceless videos are great filler clips and content; they just don't tend to go as viral for me.

- **Relevancy:** Whenever I comment on something intense happening in the news that day, like the supply chain collapse, people are feeling emotional about it. They are more likely to grab their phones and comment their thoughts under it. Don't be afraid to encourage them to share their opinions in the captions by asking everyone how they feel about the news. Relevancy is a hugely important component of viral content. No one wants to engage with yesterday's social media post.

- **Shocking:** I tend to stay away from this angle, since it doesn't make sense with my brand and I don't always agree with what creators do to go viral. But shocking videos that literally shock the viewer can cause them to watch the video repeatedly. Multiple video watches are one of the key ingredients for going viral in algorithms. It's the number one metric on TikTok: rewatches.

Maintaining Viral Momentum

Let's say you have a video go viral. Your engagement stats are exploding, and thousands of people are following you. Take advantage of this momentum. Go Live daily and welcome your new followers. Post more videos, respond to commenters every day on the viral video, and repost it to other social media apps. You want to capitalize on your hard work and have it work two or three times over for you.

Many times on TikTok, if I have a video that is going viral, there are more people visiting my profile than normal. It will kick-start a second viral video at the same time. I try to get the initial viral video to kick-start three or four more viral videos so that the virality continues for five to six weeks at a time. I do this so I can sit back and relax for a month knowing my course sales are going through the roof. During this period, I reevaluate what is going viral on the app and make new content I plan to unveil once the virality dies down.

Note that I manage to achieve this kind of virality two to three times per year. I do not have this happening on my accounts monthly. If you do not experience viral momentum during your first few months building a personal brand, that's perfectly fine. Do not let it deter you from carrying on and trying again.

Monetizing the Virality

Going viral comes with its own high. Watching the followers pour onto your accounts can almost seem like an out-of-body experience. All these new people are looking to you to entertain or educate them. They like you enough to follow you. And they possibly like you enough to click on the link in your bio.

You can take one of two routes with what you put in the link section of each social media app:

- Direct link to either an online course, online store, book, etc.
- Linktree (Linktr.ee): A Linktree allows you to link to tons of different links in one organized page. Many creators use this if they have multiple products and course offerings for their followers.

I personally have a direct link to my online course program because that is my focus for sales currently. I may at some point in the future switch over to a Linktree as I create more products for opt-ins for my followers.

As we covered in Chapter 9, you can use freelancers to make ebooks and ecommerce products for your brand. You can also record your own online courses, or partner with someone else, and sell them through your accounts. Viral content is one of the best (and freest) ways to rev up sales on your side hustles. That's why creating a personal brand on social media ties freelancing and side hustling together—it becomes one of the most powerful traffic sources for anything you want to sell.

Now that you know what to do and how to make money online, it's time to finish this book with a final part on financial freedom. We are going to look at how to invest your surplus cash, how to see yourself as a financially free person, setting up systems that work in your place, scaling to seven-plus side hustles, and finally, how to create a financially free tribe that is supportive of your hard work and desires to retire early. The journey to financial freedom is just as much one of picking and setting up side hustles as it is a mindset overhaul in which you start to see yourself for the financially fierce person you deserve to be. No longer being bound by bills or monetary concerns will thrust you into a new mental space, one that requires you to surround yourself with other financial freedom pursuers.

So, without further ado, it's time to move onto the last part of this book.

Chapter 21 Key Points

- Research is one of the fastest ways to identify how to go viral on social media.
- Viral-worthy content tends to follow relevancy, shock and awe, personalization, and controversy.
- Viral momentum can send additional videos viral on your accounts.
- Have a plan in place for how you plan to capitalize from virality with the links in your bios.

IV Financial Freedom

22 Key Concepts for Investing Your Money

A lot of people with high IQs are terrible investors because they've got terrible temperaments. You need to keep raw, irrational emotion under control.

— Charlie Munger

With more money comes more responsibility. I learned this the hard way in 2018 when an article in CNBC extensively broke down the money I was making. Messages from financial planners from around the world poured into my email inbox. People tried to "catch me" in a lie, asking me questions about how I was investing the money to prove to themselves I must be telling tall tales. At 25 years old, with very little financial education in my pocket after completing a degree in political science, I really didn't know what to do with the money. But I knew I had a responsibility to do something with it—if I could figure out how to earn it, then dammit, I was going to figure out how to invest it.

My solution was doing nothing with it for another two to three years. Yes, you can cringe all you want. I left hundreds of thousands of dollars in checking accounts. I know how inflation works, and I know I wasn't growing my money by doing that. But I had an awareness that I did not have the financial investment maturity I needed to invest it in a way that felt comfortable to me. And looking back, I am so happy I listened to my gut and took my time, as opposed to rushing into investing. Most of the "advice" I was given would have prevented me from becoming a real estate investor today.

I quickly learned that investing isn't as intimidating, emotional, or chaotic as the financial world likes to make it seem. In fact, much like "learning the stock market," a lot of investing information is gate-kept behind fancy terms, redundant calculations, and an aggressive industry designed to deter the everyday person from managing their own money. If you are smart and driven enough to make your own money, I promise you that you are also smart enough to invest it in a way that is right for you and your monetary goals.

One of the best side effects of this whole freelancing and side hustle journey is that you're going to have surplus money. It might not be in the first month or even the first year. But if you stick with it, the money will come. And when the money comes, I want you to feel confident in your management of it. I don't want you to succumb to the fearmongering that will arrive at your doorstep when a distant friend or relative catches wind that you're earning $5,000+ per month. They are going to have opinions—believe me. And unfortunately, if you're a woman (even worse, if you're a young woman), just about every person in your life is going to assume you need help managing that money—ironically, studies show that women make more prudent investors than men (Dore 2021).

That's why I want to go over three key concepts when it comes to investing and managing your newfound money. Remember: it's *your* money that *you* earned at the end of the day.

Note: I am not a licensed financial advisor and am not providing concrete financial investment advice in this chapter. I am explaining my personal experience with investing, in hopes that it can help you make the right decisions for your money.

Investing Is Personal

Growing up, I was always under the impression that there were a few "right ways" to invest money. If the wrong ways were chosen, a person could end up losing all their money. It was this concept that always made me scared of managing money, much less investing it. If I could make some wrong decisions and effectively evaporate my life savings, what was I going to do?

Boy, that concept could not be more wrong. In fact, with the pace of innovation today, the investment opportunities available to us are exponentially increasing by the day. The investment options we can access right now were not available 10, much less 30 years ago. Listening to the advice from your elders when it comes to investing can be valuable from a moral and integrity standpoint. But investing is a personal pursuit that no one else, from any other generation, can accurately advise you on. They will have their thoughts and opinions, and as I said, from a moral compass point of view, these thoughts can be greatly valuable. But at the end of the day, when it's you and those numbers in your bank account, it's a very personal decision that should be for you to make free from judgment.

For me, as the financial opinions shouted at me to get into the stock market, open high-yield savings accounts, and invest in a 401(k) (these are all perfectly fine investment options—they just didn't work with my personal investment plan), I felt that same voice in the back of my head tell me the same thing—no. I've never been someone who works for the long term. I live in the present. I like to personally access my money as I want to, and not have to wait 30 years for it to hit a maturity point in a bank account. Who says I will even be here in 30 years?

These traditional investment methods just didn't resonate with me. Lots of people whispered I was making a "mistake." It was hard for a few years to feel like many adults were snickering that I was too young to know how to manage money. But, for the first time in my investing life, I felt a tug on my heart to make my first big purchase towards the end of 2020. I didn't know if I should start investing in real estate yet, or what I was supposed to do. But I heard a voice say to me one day while I was heading to my home in Albany, New York, "buy a car." (If you listen, God gives us direction on things when we don't know what else to do.) I didn't have a car at the time since I was living in New York City. But I listened, and I bought a Jeep Wrangler in all cash. For the investment wizzes out there, that nearly gave them a heart attack. "A Jeep, in all cash? Are you crazy? Do you know how much money you would save taking out a loan instead?" I knew the difference, yet I didn't care. I wanted the Jeep paid off, in cash.

Little did I know that having the Jeep paid off in cash would make it easier for me in March 2021 to buy my first home in southwest Florida. Buying something tangible that I could use really resonated with me on an investment level. I went on to buy an investment apartment in Miami later that year, putting

20% down on both properties and taking out the rest in a loan. I am considering adding one or two more investment properties this year as well. I even completed my real estate licensing exam last week (at the time of writing), so I can make the most informed investment decisions possible when it comes to real estate.

I am also putting my money into cryptocurrency, a self-employment pension fund, and an IRA. Why? Because these investment options work best for me.

Investing is a very personal pursuit. You do not owe it to anyone to tell them about how you are investing. You also do not need to listen to unsolicited advice when it comes to investing. It's just you and the hard-earned dollars you worked so hard to attract.

If You Can Make It, You Can Invest It

Like with all the side hustle endeavors I have gone over in this book, you need some level of confidence to engage in investing properly. You need to feel confident about how you choose to manage your money. As I mentioned, you don't owe it to anyone to tell them how the money is being managed. But you do owe it to yourself to be proud and confident in the places and avenues you choose to leverage.

If you're wondering where that confidence is going to come from, I am going to explain how I was able to develop my own money management confidence.

I believe it is much harder to make money than it is to invest it. Anyone can throw their money into different bank accounts. Not everyone can set up a freelancing business, make extra money, and launch passive income streams. You're already at the finish line, in my opinion, if you can make surplus income. You already know how money works much more than the average person. You already know that creating value, attending to clients, and being in a state of gratitude can attract money to you.

It's that very concept that also guarantees that you can invest those same dollars. It's your money at the end of the day that you attracted into your business through different means. Money is merely an energy source in the world that changes hands, companies, and nations. It flows to those who put out the energy to receive it. I won't dive too deeply into the psychology of money, but if you are attracting it in abundance, you already know what to do with it.

Be stubborn with this concept. If anyone tries to make you second-guess your decision, remind them that you were able to set up, launch, and grow a freelancing business without their input. You can say it more nicely if you want—when you get to where I am and thousands of unsolicited opinions later, you just say it like it is.

The World of Investing Is Gate-Kept with Intimidation Tactics

This is a very real thing I didn't realize was so pervasive until I dove headfirst into business. All the investment jargon and the Wall Street stock market culture make people feel like they are outsiders to investing. I felt it, too! It wasn't until I started to really break down my own approach to money that I realized these gate-keeping tactics are just that—they're invisible walls.

There are no barriers preventing you from investing. It benefits the financial industry to make people feel that they need the support, advice, and financial products they offer to invest wisely. It's all BS!

Once you realize the intimidation is just a byproduct of an industry that will do whatever it can to make money off your success, you will realize that you have the power to invest. It's an empowering thing when you start to see intimidation tactics from a mile away (they unfortunately litter just about every major industry in the world today). I won't go into the history of why these tactics exist in the first place because I do not wish to alienate men or women from this discussion, but I do want you to be aware that if financial jargon makes you feel insecure, please know that you are not alone.

Change will come when we all start to move collectively past the gate-keeping and manage our money personally. If you go on to tell even one person today about what you learned in this chapter, the change will be tangible. Financial literacy and education are at the foundation, I believe, of every single person changing the current socioeconomic class that they are in. Learning that investing is a personal, inherent, and simplistic pursuit is one of the most valuable things you can do in the management of your money.

Behind your investing confidence and personal money management is a mindset that will need to push you through the criticism and unwarranted opinions. The saying "mindset is everything" is true. It's been truer than anything else in my money journey. Getting your headspace into a place where you believe you deserve the money you are earning and that you have the power to invest wisely is critical—and it's what we're going to cover in the next chapter.

Chapter 22 Key Points

- Investing is a highly personal pursuit that should be private to you.

- New investment opportunities that were not around for generations past are created every day.

- If you are smart enough to earn money, you are smart enough to invest it.

- Don't let intimidation tactics keep you from personalized investing.

23 Seeing Yourself as a Financially Free Person

When you understand that your self-worth is not determined by your net worth, then you'll have financial freedom.

— Suze Orman

You are what you think. Everything you have in your life right now started as a thought in your brain. You either chose to act on that thought or not. You either chose to believe you could act on that thought or not. Philosophers for thousands of years have known and written about this. For example, the Roman emperor Marcus Aurelius penned, "A man's life is what his thoughts make of it." Ralph Waldo Emerson stated, "A man is what he thinks about all day long" (Itani 2020).

This mindset hack will change your life in everything that you do. But for the purposes of this chapter, we are going to talk about shifting your mindset into one where you comfortably see yourself not only as a financially free person—but as someone who *deserves* financial freedom.

A very common side effect from years of piled-on trauma, criticisms, and improperly placed blame and/or doubt can leave people feeling that they are not deserving of wealth, much less success. We come to believe all the negative things we have been told we are throughout our lives. The people who have blamed or doubted us make us feel that we are not deserving of anything good. It's a very normal psychological response that most people must wrestle with when shifting into a money mindset. Do not feel bad about yourself if you feel a mental abundance roadblock. Now is the time to start cheering yourself on and envisioning a future of financial freedom that you deserve.

So, how do you start to see yourself as this champion of financial freedom? Of living a life in which worrying about your next dollar is a thing of the past? From a mindset perspective, I want you to consider the following process.

Step 1: Acknowledging Your Current Wealth Roadblocks

This is undoubtedly the hardest step in shifting your mindset into one of positive financial freedom reception. It's going deep into the corners of your mind and unearthing different belief systems that you have come to adopt as a result of trauma. Maybe, without realizing it, you speak negatively to yourself every day. Maybe you have convinced yourself you will never be wealthy because "being rich is something that doesn't happen to people like me." Maybe you are afraid of success, and on some level, accountability and responsibility. Whatever it may be, you need to do some work to identify it first.

Here are a few ways you can go about doing this:

- Spend some time alone on a walk. Consider solo yoga or health retreats. Silent meditation groups can be powerful as well. Unplug when you work out, turn off the music, and leave your phone at home. Start thinking about your thoughts and notice them as they come in and out of your mind (the foundation of meditation). Take your time and be patient with yourself.

- Consider seeing a therapist. Therapists can be invaluable in helping you identify thought patterns you didn't even realize you used every day. It can be incredibly challenging to see ourselves with unemotional clarity.

- Grab a journal and start writing. Write down things that have hurt you in the past. Write down your beliefs. Write down your passions. Keep writing and notice commonalities and groupings. You will start to see patterns in what you think, and what you want. Spend some time, again, doing this and be patient with yourself.

I never advocate for you to explore possibly very hurtful trauma that can be painful to unearth alone. If you feel you need support through this, please seek out loved ones, partners, and therapists to be there with you. Go at a pace that feels right for you, even if it's just five minutes of meditating in the morning when you wake up. Having awareness of what your mental roadblocks are and where they come from will completely transform your life.

When it comes to the attraction of wealth and money, specifically, inside of our minds, we can speak barriers into existence without even realizing it. Some wealth roadblocks can look and sound like this:

- I am too stupid to be wealthy.
- I am too poor to be wealthy.
- I was not born into a wealthy family; therefore, I will never be wealthy.

- I will never amount to anything.
- I am not someone who has good luck.
- I am not someone who has good things happen to me.
- I am not deserving of money.
- I don't have any talents.
- I don't know how to make money.
- I was not born in the right country to be wealthy.
- I was not born the right gender/class/race to be wealthy.
- I am not good at learning.

Once you have an awareness of these roadblocks, you can start to unpack them. No person is "too far gone" when it comes to rewiring your brain. Your mind is so much more vastly impressive and complex than you can even comprehend. It can do whatever you need it to do. But that starts with you having a desire to make the change.

Step 2: Using Manifestation and Affirmations

At this point, you have some basic understanding of negative thought patterns that are blocking financial attraction. With this information, you can start to rewire the very thoughts that come in and out of your brain. You can literally change them, and it starts with two powerful practices. These practices have different names depending on the study and religion. For the purpose of this book, we are going to call them manifestation and affirmations.

Manifestation is the art of making your goals come true. It's a technique based on the Law of Attraction, which states that you can have whatever you want in your life if you attract it to yourself. This theory posits that our brains can act as magnets to our desires if we believe that we truly can make them a reality. It's stating out loud whatever it is that you want to achieve and picturing yourself achieving it repeatedly in your head. It's clearing any ounce of self-doubt and feeling 100% in belief that you are going to make it happen.

Affirmations are the building blocks of manifesting a goal or dream. Affirmations are statements in which you envision and believe that something is going to happen. It's writing down in a journal every morning: "I am wealthy. I am whole. I am deserving of success. I am successful. I am in pursuit of my dreams. I am healing." It's making a statement as if something has already come to pass, which can help to rewire the brain to manifest whatever it is that you want in your life.

Now before anyone tells me this is getting a little woo-woo, studies have proven that positive thoughts bring more success and other positive people into a person's life (Mnich 2021). Additionally, at the basis of manifestation is still the need to act and put the work in to make it happen. Simply thinking it and never doing anything from your home will not make your financial freedom dreams come true. But thinking it, first, is an important part of kick-starting the entire process.

For manifestation and affirmations, journals can be great tools to track it, write it down, and reflect on it weeks from now. Many people choose to journal in either the morning or evening (or both). They also keep food journals, dream journals, and fitness journals, and you can do this too if you find those elements help on your journey of self-love and acceptance. Forming financial freedom groups can be a great idea as well (we will touch on this in-depth in Chapter 26).

So long as you are moving forward, even if it's baby steps every day, with how you talk to yourself and plan your goals, you will be well on your way to making this mindset a reality for yourself.

Step 3: Having Gratitude

The final element in keeping a financial freedom mindset is managing it in the present. You are going to have good and bad things happen to you. Sometimes, that side hustle or that PayPal transfer isn't going to be what you thought it would be. You may have great seasons with your business, and then financial pitfalls that you did not see coming. How are you going to make sure you keep your head in that positive place where you continue to talk with encouragement inside of your mind? The answer stems from one thing: gratitude.

If you commit yourself to being grateful, every single day, for what you have and what you are doing, I promise you will never lose sight of this new kind of thinking. In that same journal, write down five things you are grateful for every single day. Read them over and really think about them. Reflect on them if you go on a walk. Give back to the world—post on social media and help other people change their mindsets, too. Share wisdom and tips for how you made your side hustle a reality. Donate to charities or start your own. Volunteer and spend some time helping others without a monetary profit at the end of it.

Rooting your mindset in a place of gratefulness above all else will make you infallible. If you had the money to buy this book and you can read these words, that's something to be grateful for. If you have a roof over your head and you don't have to fear for your safety every day, that's something to be grateful for. Never forget why you embarked on this journey in the first place and be grateful that you have had the awakening needed to change your financial life. The rest will fall into place.

Now that you are ready to sharpen your most powerful weapon, your mind, and you know what to do, it's time to talk about setting up systems that work in your place. It's time to change your mindset from focusing specifically on active income, trading time for money, and advancing to a place of passive income, or making money in your sleep. Now that you know you are worthy and deserving of such income and such freedom, let's get down to it.

Chapter 23 Key Points

- You are deserving of financial freedom and enjoyment.
- Everyone has wealth roadblocks—slowly start to work through yours.
- Grab a journal and start practicing manifestation and affirmations, mixed with hard work.
- Root your mind in gratefulness and you will never feel the need to revert to negative thinking again.

24 The Benefits of Systems That Work in Your Place

It's not how much money you make, but how much money you keep, how hard it works for you, and how many generations you keep it for.

— Robert Kiyosaki

When it comes to financial freedom, at its rawest core is the need to switch from active to passive income in as many areas of your business as possible. Trading time for money is where we all must start. Building up freelancing businesses that turn into side hustle empires starts with active income. I was steeped in nothing but active income for the first five years of my journey, and I wouldn't change it for the world.

But at some point, you're going to have a thought: What if I could make this money in my sleep? What if you could work half of the hours you currently are, and make the same money, if not more? This is the thought that pops into every single millionaire's and billionaire's brain in the world. They talk to each other about passive income in passing, like it's a normal, logical element of their businesses that's needed to scale it to the billions. They already know the financial freedom secret, while the rest of us complete our schooling and receive training at corporations that don't ever dare touch the concept of passive income.

But these billionaires, too, came from a place of not knowing at some point. They made the decision to reject what society was telling them and uncover the secret we are talking about right now. Can you fault them for it? They were—and are—playing the same game we all are. We should focus our energy on breaking out of the matrix just the way that they did, starting with passive income systems that work in their place. In Chapter 25, we will go over the magic seven streams of income rule, and why these billionaires all have multiple streams of income. For right now, we are going to look at the benefits of passive income: the most basic way to make that dream of financial freedom a powerful reality for yourselves in the months to come.

Believing You Can Make the Switch to Passive Income

I will start by saying that not everything can be switched to a passive income model. But just about everything can be automated with virtual assistants and software, so that you only need to check in on the business a few times every month. In a lot of ways, that's making a business passive, and it can be done with the most active of business models, like managing a freelancing business.

To monitor a successful passive income pivot requires you to first believe it's possible. We must shed the idea that successful businesses can only be run by CEOs with executive assistants and slews of employees. We are living in a very fast-paced and technologically chaotic time, which—although it does have bad side effects—brings with it the ability to automate and make passive many businesses that previously required active management. So many new software, artificial intelligence (AI), and automation tools are popping up every single day that they could never be up to date in any book you read. The pace at which they are being thrust into the open digital marketplace is hard for even the smartest person to wrap their brain around. The good news is: you don't have to keep up with the pace of innovative releases; you just need to be positively open to the changes and receptive to new tools that land in your email inbox.

For years, I fought this innovation. I traded time for money. I traded so much time that I was working 60-plus-hour weeks, fighting the feeling in my gut that it was time to expand and let go of the control. I switched over to passive income with my freelancing business by hiring a person to be me, essentially, with a team below her that she manages on the day-to-day. I am only contacted for problems the team cannot solve without my input. In Chapters 12–14, we looked at the power of virtual assistants, paired with freelancers, and how just about any business can switch over to this freelancing agency model (covered in Chapter 4).

I am now applying this model to other facets of my business, like my influencing and sponsorship packages. I have hired an influencing management company that handles emails, invoicing, follow-ups, negotiations, and contracts with brands. All I have to do is show up, read the script, and film the content. They take 20%, yet I have about 95% of my time back. This tradeoff is common with turning any business into passive income, since the software tools will cost something. In the grand scheme of life, these tools will cost 1–2% of the money they are able to bring in for you, without the human error. They pay for themselves, and then some, especially in the form of peace of mind.

The Point of Passive No Return

There will come a time when your systems are in place and you are ready to step back and see how they do. It's going to be an exhilarating, stressful, and necessary time on your quest for financial freedom. You will have to step back and trust that your team, which is mainly comprised of technology, can do the job for you.

But it doesn't have to be a "do or die" moment. You can step back and allow the systems to run while monitoring them every single day if you want. You can watch what your team is saying in Slack, you can log in to the different software tools and check the analytics, and you can read over client feedback. You can be just as involved as you were previously—or you can enjoy your newfound time back. Over time, you will come to trust these systems and be able to unplug. Once you go on that first trip halfway around the world and make a couple of thousand dollars while never checking your phone, you will never have that passive income anxiety ever again.

We all need that push at some point. We need to jump off the cliff to learn we can fly. You've already done this so many times before, with different side hustles and freelancing. This is just the final jump between you and making passive income, and therefore financial freedom, a tangible commodity.

The Money-Retention Balancing Act

The quote in the beginning of this chapter is from Robert Kiyosaki, who wrote one of my favorite business books, *Rich Dad, Poor Dad*. This book is all about retaining the money you already have and investing it in a way that lowers your taxable income. As opposed to worrying about where the money is coming from, Robert urges readers to consider the active management of the money coming in and how they can trim the fat to prevent the money going out.

You're going to need to try out different software tools and programs until you find ones that work for you and are set at the right price point. Some of them may rack up $500/month and only bring in $1,000. Others may cost you only $100 yet bring in just $50. You are going to need to play around with the tools available to you. The good news is that there are so many software tools out there right now, that I can promise you, there are ones perfectly suited for your current business. But Rome wasn't built in a day, which is why you are going to need that same patience I challenged you to use earlier in this book, to create these final financial freedom systems.

Robert would argue that it's a good idea at this point to sit down with a CPA who has tax planning advice and go over these systems with them. They will be able to provide you with feedback and suggestions on different avenues you can take to lower your tax burden. Financial freedom isn't possible without a tax planning strategy that ensures you can finally live without concerning yourself over the source of your money.

It's truly an extraordinary time to be alive and do business in the world right now. I can't stress that enough. The fact that you can set up systems, online, that you own 100%, and that you can automate to make you money in your sleep is incredible. I don't want anyone to take it for granted—I sure don't. Being appreciative of these tools will help you attract even more abundance into your online business. Remember: you are what you think.

Next, let's look at the diversification of income streams, and why the average millionaire has seven sources of money. They know better than anyone that in order to live financially free, there need to be multiple monetary options. You never know when one is going to collapse or become mundane, especially in a world with a volatile economy.

Chapter 24 Key Points

- Setting up passive income systems is the quickest way to financial freedom.
- Most businesses can be made passive, but not all.
- You will hit a point at which you have to step back and allow tools/people to run your businesses for you.
- Always do a cost-benefit analysis with the tools you are onboarding to ensure you are retaining as much money as possible.

25 The "Seven Streams of Income" Rule

The most powerful form of wealth-building today isn't about earning a paycheck; it's about what you know.

— T. Harv Eker

I received both a high school and college education that emphasized the importance of finding one source of reliable income. It was subliminally marketed to us from the moment we sat down in high school economics class, to when the political science department at my college anxiously asked me where I "planned to work" after graduation so they could boast about the success of their students to other professors.

The idea of pursuing not one, not two, but multiple streams of income was nowhere to be found. If someone had suggested such a thing, both the class and the educators would have probably snickered. I caused a lot of snickering in my college classes for going against the grain. My alternative approach to political philosophy and the study of history was sometimes welcomed—only if it fit the narrative of the professor. Watching my curiosity annoy quite a few educators told me something powerful: I was teetering on the edge of discovering something big. Questioning the working world for its obsession with just one stream of income unknowingly launched me into the world of freelancing. It's funny when you can reflect on all of it years later, seeing that nothing, ever, is a coincidence.

As I learned more and more about this remote working economy and the potential of taking on a side hustle, I began to read a lot of books. At some point in their pages, they would all reference this "seven streams of income" rule. I would think to myself: "Wow, seven?!" And here I thought I was a revolutionary for suggesting the average person pursue two to three streams of income.

Just think of how stark of a contrast that is, when you compare just one stream of income to seven. No wonder millionaires and billionaires end up pulling further and further ahead of the average person with their wealth accumulation. I realized these people don't play by the same set of rules as most of the population. But I didn't sit there and hate them for it. I figured, "Wow, these people know something I don't, and it's clearly working for them." Let's see what it's all about (shifting your mind into a place where you pause and react with rationality—before emotional resentment kicks in—will do wonders for you in the world of business).

It was this very inspiration that motivated me to try out my first few additional streams of income to freelancing on Fiverr. It started with my ebooks, and moved its way into online courses, content creation, and well, you know the rest. The more streams of income I added, the more confident I felt that I would never face a situation in which the flow of money just "disappeared." I had that same fear, too, starting out as a freelancer, relying just on Fiverr. But as my income streams surpassed five, and then seven, and then 10, I began to realize the more diversified and extensive your income sources are, the more invincible you will become. And so began my obsession with telling every person I can about the seven streams of income rule.

How Do We Know the Average Millionaire Has Seven Streams of Income?

The IRS decided to get to the bottom of what makes the average millionaire by conducting a study that reviewed tax returns from the years 1996 to 2002 (Bourne and Rosenmerkel n.d.). The IRS looked at a sample of 6,053 individuals who died during this time period, while also factoring in the work of Tom Corley, who studied millionaires as well, during a five-year period.

The IRS found that wealthy people build up to seven streams of income to diversify their money, create tax shelters, and protect themselves against unforeseen market changes. Diversified income would ensure that if one or two income streams were taken out by a market collapse or dissolution, the other remaining streams of income could pick up the slack. Tax shelters, or legal ways to withhold having to pay tax on earned income by way of real estate and investing, were another motive for the multiple streams of income. If one business reported a gain, and the other a loss, or by way of depreciation in real estate investments, the person would be able to lower their final taxable income for that year. Lastly, millionaires had weathered their fair share of market changes and knew how to guard against them.

I have attempted to conduct similar studies through polls in my Instagram Stories. I have come to similar conclusions, finding that almost every person under the age of 30 who classifies themselves as a millionaire on my social media has at least seven streams of income. And, when considering that this study looked at a time frame a couple of decades ago, I would be willing to bet the income stream number has increased drastically with the arrival of AI and automation. One business, like making content on social media, can generate multiple income streams (course sales, ebook sales, affiliate links, sponsorships, ad revenue, and so on).

What Are the Seven Streams of Income?

I have mainly focused on active and passive income for the purposes of this book. But that does not encapsulate every form of income in the world. In this same study done by the IRS, they broke down the different forms of income they observed in wealthy individuals' tax returns. They are as follows:

1. Investment income: income from stocks owned.
2. Earned income: payments from employment.
3. Rental income: rental payments from tenants.
4. Royalty income: payments from selling rights to use something that has been created or invented.
5. Capital gains: from selling appreciated assets.
6. Profits: income after expenses were accounted for in any kind of business.
7. Interest income: money that's accrued from bonds, CDs, or other forms of lending.

Currently, I own investment income, rental income, royalty income, soon-to-be capital gains, and profits. But I have multiple forms of profits coming from different corners of the internet. Profit was my first form of income on my own. I soon added on investment income, then royalty income, followed now by rental and capital gains.

You do not have to follow or mimic how I have chosen to diversify my income. There is no one right way to do it. But the studies do not lie: diversifying how and where your money comes from is a commonality among all successful financial freedom aficionados.

How to Get Started Chasing the Lucky Seven

As mentioned, there are many different paths to hitting that lucky number seven, and no single one is the "ultimate" right way to make it happen. I can only go over how I was able to make it happen for myself, since I can vouch for its success and effectiveness. The following pursuit of the seven streams lines up perfectly with the structure of this book, starting with freelancing, and then side hustles, followed by investing.

- **Step 1: Prioritize Earned Income and Profits**

  I went down the profits route by opening a Fiverr account and scaling it as quickly as possible. In your case, that may be working as a freelancer for an already established agency, thereby qualifying you as an employee. You could also possibly work for an agency and freelance using a platform on the side. There are far fewer rules in the remote work economy—and that's why I love it. Work on opening two to three different forms of income in this first step.

- **Step 2: Investment Time**

  Once you really hit your profitable flow, set some of that money aside and invest it. Place it in accounts, real estate, cryptocurrencies . . . wherever you feel called. Just make sure it's making you some money every month without ever having to touch it.

- ### Step 3: Double Up with Royalties

  Royalty income embodies most passive income today. This should be a huge focus of yours for financial freedom.

  I consider my courses to be royalty income, since I charge a subscription price every month to give people access to the courses until they decide to cancel their membership. This is where you stop trading time for money, along with your investment income, to really start to build out that empire.

- ### Step 4: Rental Income and Capital Gains

  I have been investing in real estate for the multitude of monetary and tax benefits that comes with it. Depreciation can lower your taxable income, appreciation can increase the amount of money you will get when you sell the property down the line, rental income can become highly passive if you opt to use a management company, and overall real estate comes with more tax breaks than I should probably explain since I am not a CPA.

- ### Step 5: Consider Interest Income

  Last, as for interest income, although I do not currently pursue this type of income, that does not mean you should avoid it. Try it out at steps 2–4 and see what it can do for you. There is no harm in having a desire to build out your business and expand where your money comes from.

Our society has demonized this in recent years as being greedy or capitalist of you. It's merely leveraging from the systems in place and working with a tax code that rewards the creation of businesses, jobs, and housing. There is nothing wrong with wanting more for yourself and to create a reality in which you live free from money woes. We all want to break out of the matrix, but we must be pragmatic to make that a reality.

Before I wrap this book up, I want to touch on a very important concept, especially in the social and spiritual realm. While you are in hot pursuit to become a beacon of hope in the world of financial freedom, you are going to need a community that supports you. You are not meant to do any of this alone. What's the point of total financial freedom if you can't share it with the people who mean the most to you? Let's look at building your financial freedom tribe.

Chapter 25 Key Points

- The IRS confirmed that the average millionaire has at least seven streams of income.
- There are seven very different kinds of income that, when combined, can set you financially free.
- There is no one right way to diversify your income—if you pursue diversification altogether, you will be all set.
- Remember to take your time and invest your money in a way that feels right to you.

26 Building Your Financial Freedom Tribe

My favorite things in life don't cost any money. It's really clear that the most precious resource we all have is time.

— Steve Jobs

We are highly social beings, no matter how many times we try to tell ourselves that we do better alone. When we are with other people, we share mirror neurons that let us match each other's emotions; we anticipate other's movements when we're in agreement; and we can even mirror each other's brain activity when we are doing things like telling stories and listening (Morgan 2015).

Putting all that fancy scientific jargon aside—we thrive when we are in communities. That's why humans have been congregating together in towns, tribes, and villages for thousands of years. We know that spiritually, physically, and emotionally we need to be around other people to really reach our peak potential. No matter how much technology we have at our fingertips today, we still have that same primal craving. It's why so many people have a social media addiction—we can't get enough from the people around us.

I believe society's recent harsh shift into idealizing solitude is a dangerous thing for emotional and mental health. You can't deny that spending time with people you love, laughing, smiling, telling stories, dancing, and singing doesn't fill up your soul. The best things in the entire world don't come with a price tag, but we can experience more of them on a regular basis if we set ourselves free, first, from the financial burden of existing in the twenty-first century.

Everything I have detailed and asked of you in this book is possible. But that doesn't mean you need to do it all alone. In fact, I recommend that you not attempt to do everything I have described thus far in total isolation. This has been something I have struggled with over the last decade, trying to hide my success and ambitions from the people around me who I knew would not be supportive. In my most recent years I have finally caved and allowed myself to welcome in other like-minded people who don't find it funny at all when I tell them I want to be financially retired by age 33. And, boy, once you get a taste of that, you're never going to go back to entrepreneurial isolation again.

Finding these like-minded people is not always easy. But if you've made it this far in my story, then I can trust you are up for the challenge.

It Starts by Envisioning and Attracting Your Ideal Tribe

Back in Chapter 23, we talked about manifestation and the law of attraction. Well, these concepts hold true for attracting the people you want into your inner circle (spoiler alert, these concepts hold true for getting anything you want in this lifetime, but I'll leave that for my next book). You need to first sit down, perhaps again with that journal, and start envisioning your life six months from now. Who do you see sitting around you? Who do you want to spend your time with? What new characteristics do you crave in these people that you are not getting from your current friends?

It's okay to be brutally honest with yourself during this process. It doesn't mean you need to drop all your previous friends who don't share in your financial freedom drive. For the longest time, I thought it would be "disloyal" of me to bring in these new people who were just like me. I am a very stubbornly loyal person (I am the captain who goes down with the ship), so I did not want to do anything that could possibly hurt the already amazing people in my circle of friends and family.

But with time, I have realized it's not disloyal at all to create a financial freedom tribe curated exactly to you. We are the sum of our five closest friends (Antonopoulos 2016). We come to think, talk, and act just as they do—that's how malleable we are to the people in our close-knit community. That can be an incredibly powerful, and dangerous, realization. If you surround yourself with negative thinkers, people who make fun of your dreams, and friends who whisper behind your back, you will start to mirror those emotions. It's okay to be selfish in this moment and curate a community of people who support you and your positive endeavors.

Give yourself creative license to start writing down the kind of people you want in your tribe. Really close your eyes and think about what they are like, what they say, and how they think. The more specific you can be in this visualization, the easier it will become to attract these people to you.

Where Do You Find These Inspiring People?

You've spent time envisioning your tribe. Now for the hard part: where the heck are you going to go find these people? Where are other financial freedom fairies who wake up every day with a desire to change the world for the better?

From my personal experience, my social media has been the most powerful tool for finding my tribe. By putting my authentic self, beliefs, and goals on my social media, dozens of other creators have connected with me based on who I unequivocally am. These online relationships have turned into in-person friendships, travel trips, and connections to even more amazing people. I have also found going to areas in the United States where I feel a spiritual pull to go typically means they are teeming with people I need in my life (shout-out to God for constantly giving us a nudge to do what is best in our lives). For example, this past year, I was feeling an intense pull to go to Austin, Texas. I listened, went for four weeks, and made pivotal business and friendship connections there. It felt like home immediately.

I have also heard of other businesspeople using the dating app Bumble with it set to friends mode. You can create Facebook groups, retreats, Meet-up groups, and so forth to foster collaboration among yourself and other people who are just like you. They are out there, I promise. Thanks to social media, it's easier than ever for you two to find each other. It just might take a little time. Everything happens for a reason.

Welcoming in Others Down the Line

I will always believe in paying it forward. I believe that putting good energy out there, sharing your wisdom with others, and being in a selfless place not only makes the world a better place, but it makes you happy, too. We were created with an intense yearning to give back and connect with others. That yearning never goes away, no matter how successful or wealthy you might be. If you remember to be grateful and pay it forward, you are always going to enjoy this process.

A few years from now, some entrepreneurs online may try to reach out to you and ask to meet you. They may want to grab coffee with your tribe. They may just want a piece of advice. You and I are never too important to slow down and help someone. I still review my direct messages, respond to as many comments as possible, post charities for free on my social media, and donate weekly. You and I aren't "better" than most of the population because we have this whole financial freedom thing down. If anything, we have a responsibility now to go out into the world and share what we have learned with others.

And that is exactly what I hope I have done with you in this book. I have so much more I want to share with you, and I want you to know how proud I am of you for reading this kind of book. It means you have a desire to want more for your life. You have a desire to change the world, one step at a time. You don't believe you're just sitting on a rock hurling through outer space, but that there is a purpose to everything down here.

Regardless of where you are on your financial freedom journey, keep going. We're only in the very beginning stages of a work movement that is much bigger than you and I. You can freelance your way to freedom, I promise. See you soon.

Chapter 26 Key Points

- You can't do this alone—be vulnerable enough to admit that to yourself.

- We are the sum of the five people we surround ourselves with.

- Being authentic and true to yourself will help attract your financial freedom tribe.

- Never be too good to pass it forward—you have a responsibility to go out there and tell someone else about the world of financial freedom.

REFERENCES

Afshar, Vala. 2021. "AI-Powered Virtual Assistants and the Future of Work." *ZDnet*, April 7, https://www.zdnet.com/article/ai-powered-virtual-assistants-and-future-of-work/.

Antonopoulos, Alexandra. 2016. "Why You Should Reevaluate Who Your 5 Closest Friends Are in 2017." *Elite Daily*, December 18, https://www.elitedaily.com/life/sum-of-5-closest-friends/1723824.

Aslam, Salman. 2022. "51 Pinterest Statistics You Need to Know in 2022." *Omnicore*, January 4, https://www.omnicoreagency.com/pinterest-statistics/.

Booth, Barbara. 2019. "Skilled Freelancers, Earning More Per Hour than 70% of Workers in US, Don't Want Traditional Jobs." CNBC, October 3, https://www.cnbc.com/2019/10/03/skilled-freelancers-earn-more-per-hour-than-70percent-of-workers-in-us.html.

Bourne, Jenny, and Lisa Rosenmerkel. n.d "Over the Top: How Tax Returns Show That the Very Rich Are Different from You and Me." Accessed March 11, 2022. https://www.irs.gov/pub/irs-soi/14rpoverthetopbournerosenmerkel.pdf.

Castrillon, Caroline. 2019. "Why Personal Branding Is More Important Than Ever." *Forbes*, February 12, https://www.forbes.com/sites/carolinecastrillon/2019/02/12/why-personal-branding-is-more-important-than-ever/?sh=7783a8c02408.

Cummins, Todd. 2021."People Spend on Average 2½ Hours a Day on Social Media." HomeTown Stations.com, October 17, https://www.hometownstations.com/news/people-spend-on-average-2-1-2-hours-a-day-on-social-media/article_76e36a88-2f72-11ec-a9b9-d7da3c499af9.html.

Dean, Brian. 2021. "Social Network Usage & Growth Statistics: How Many People Use Social Media in 2022?" *Backlinko*, October 10, https://backlinko.com/social-media-users.

Dean, Brian. 2022a. "TikTok User Statistics (2022)." *Backlinko*, January 5, https://backlinko.com/tiktok-users.

Dean, Brian. 2022b. "Twitch Usage and Growth Statistics: How Many People Use Twitch in 2022?" *Backlinko*, January 5, https://backlinko.com/twitch-users.

Dore, Kate, CFP. 2021. "Women Investors Are Still Outperforming Men, Study Finds." CNBC, October 11, https://www.cnbc.com/2021/10/11/women-investors-are-still-outperforming-men-study-finds.html.

Ellwood, Beth. 2021. "Meta-Analysis Suggests That Emotional Intelligence Is Declining Among College Students." *PsyPost*, November 9, https://www.psypost.org/2021/11/meta-analysis-suggests-that-emotional-intelligence-is-declining-among-college-students-62087.

Ferriss, Timothy. *The 4-Hour Workweek: Escape 9–5, Live Anywhere, and Join the New Rich*. New York: Crown.

Geyser, Werner. 2021. "31 Mind-Blowing Pinterest Stats for 2022." *Influencer MarketingHub*, December 29, https://influencermarketinghub.com/pinterest-stats/#:~:text=for%20their%20products.-,6.,group%20compared%20to%20 2019%20findings.

Gilbert, Elizabeth. 2015. *Big Magic: Creative Living Beyond Fear*. New York: Riverhead Books.

Goldsmith, Jill. 2021. "Facebook Hits 2.91 Billion Monthly Active Users in Q3: Earnings, Outlook Mixed Amid Advertising Headwinds." *Deadline*, October 25, https://deadline.com/2021/10/facebook-earnings-mark-zuckeberg-whistleblower-apple-1234862038/.

Itani, Omar. 2020. "You Are What You Think: How Your Thoughts Create Your Reality." *Omar Itani* (blog), April 21, https://www.omaritani.com/blog/what-you-think.

Kanwar, Karan. 2020. "Next-Generation Virtual Assistants Will Be Far Sexier Than Alexa and Siri." *Builtin.com*, May 8, https://builtin.com/software-engineering-perspectives/virtual-assistants-alexa-siri.

Kiyosaki, Robert T. 2017. *Rich Dad, Poor Dad: What the Rich Teach Their Kids About Money—That the Poor and Middle Class Do Not!* Scottsdale, AZ: Plata Publishing.

Krockow, Eva M., PhD. 2018. "Too Much Choice." *Psychology Today*, October 9, https://www.psychologytoday.com/us/blog/stretching-theory/201810/too-much-choice.

Maidan, Laila. 2021. "A 32-Year-Old Dancer Reached a $4 Million Net Worth Thanks to 5 Strategic Money Decisions." *Business Insider*, April 20, https://www.businessinsider.com/personal-finance/how-reached-four-million-dollar-net-worth-in-years-2021-4?op=1.

Martin, Susan Taylor. 2016. "Tampa Bay Is One of the Most Affordable Housing Markets, But Mortgage Rates Top Nation." *Tampa Bay Times*, March 3, https://www.tampabay.com/news/business/realestate/tampa-bay-is-one-of-the-most-affordable-housing-markets-but-mortgage-rates/2267814/#:~:text=As%20of%20last%20week%2C%20the,%2C00%20median%2Dpriced%20home.

Minton, Rob. n.d. "The 7 Income Streams of Millionaires (According to the IRS)." *Dividend Real Estate*. Accessed February 18, 2022. https://dividendrealestate.com/7incomestreams/.

Mnich, Kinga. 2021. "The Science Behind Manifestation: Does the Law of Attraction Work?" Kinga Mnich, March 25, https://kingamnich.com/2021/03/25/science-behind-law-of-attraction/.

Morgan, Nick. 2015. "We Humans Are Social Beings—And Why That Matters for Speakers and Leaders." *Forbes*, September 1, https://www.forbes.com/sites/nickmorgan/2015/09/01/we-humans-are-social-beings-and-why-that-matters-for-speakers-and-leaders/?sh=2be98f776abd.

Tannenbaum, Daniel. n.d. "Online Education and eLearning Are Projected to Reach $350 Billion by 2025," TeachThought.com. Accessed February 18, 2022. https://www.teachthought.com/the-future-of-learning/online-education/.

Younger, Jon. 2021. "The Freelance Revolution Has a Supply Problem, Not a Demand Problem." *Forbes*, December 13, https://www.forbes.com/sites/jonyounger/2021/12/13/the-freelance-revolution-has-a-supply-problem-not-a-demand-problem/?sh=7d6e71431150.

ABOUT THE AUTHOR

Alexandra Fasulo is a full-time freelance writer, Fiverr millionaire, and host of the Freelance Fairytales Podcast, a top 1% business podcast that covers the changing world of remote work, the Great Resignation, and financial freedom. She is the owner of five different online courses that cover the basics of getting started on Fiverr and making money as a copywriter, as well as the owner of Alex Fasulo LLC, a media and influencer agency that pairs Alex's brand "The Freelance Fairy" with up-and-coming remote-work brands and startups.

Alex commands a following of over 840,000 across Instagram, TikTok, YouTube, Pinterest, LinkedIn, and Facebook, as well as one of the biggest freelancing groups (24,400 members) on Facebook: Freelancing Mentorship with Alexandra Fasulo. Her story has been documented at length on CNBC, *Business Insider*, *Forbes*, *Entrepreneur*, and Yahoo!.

Alex is passionate about discussing the future of work, helping people quit their 9-to-5s and freelance full-time, and preparing people for tech developments and automation that will make tens of thousands of jobs obsolete in the coming years. She believes the remote work economy makes it easier than ever before for any person, regardless of their background or education level, to make a respectable income they can invest and live off for their rest of their lives.

INDEX